Panel

RADIO WIZARD

Radio Wizard

EDWARD SAMUEL ROGERS

and the Revolution of Communications

Ian A. Anthony

Gage Publishing Company for

ROGERS™

CANADIAN CATALOGUING IN PUBLICATION DATA

Anthony, Ian
Radio Wizard: Edward Samuel Rogers and the revolution
of communication

ISBN 7715-8050-9

1. Rogers, Edward Samuel, 1900–1939.   2. Radio – Canada – Biography.
3. Inventors – Canada – Biography.   I. Title

TK6545.R63A57 2000a   621.384'092   C00-931251-X

Publisher: Gage Educational Publishing Company,
164 Commander Blvd, Toronto, Ont. M1S 3C7
Editorial Services: Denise Schon Books Inc.
Design: Counterpunch/Linda Gustafson
Cover/Title page background image: early CFRB control room

Printed and bound in Canada by Friesens

Rogers experimental 15-S.
The world's first AC tube, 1925

Follow the dream. Accept the challenge. Put forward your best effort tirelessly with good intent and success will be your own reward.

CONTENTS

FOREWORD

I lost my father as a boy of five years old. His memory, which was kept alive by my mother, Velma Taylor Rogers, has provided me with an incredible inspiration. His discovery of the AC tube and its application for modern day broadcasting led me to a lifelong interest in the telecommunications sector. My father was an inventor and entrepreneur. He was also a proud Canadian. He started and grew his business in this country and even during tough economic times remained in, and committed, to Canada.

I, like my mother, have been proud and honoured to remember my father and his contributions. I have passed this legacy on to Loretta's and my own children, Lisa, Edward, Melinda and Martha, who, I hope, will in turn pass along to their children.

This book is one small way to keep the memory alive.

Edward S. Rogers
June 2000

Ted Rogers, 1930

A Spark Races
Through the Sky

The wonder of electric communication. Whether the staccato rhythm of a telegraph or the instantaneous flash of e mail, the expression of thought via airwaves is an astounding miracle. A message is translated into a new form, signals are relayed, there is a deciphering at the end terminal, and the message returns to its original state for the recipient. When one pauses to consider it, this is quite an amazing process. Interaction of this type transforms our vast planet into little more than a "global village," allowing society to advance with the passing of each day.

Modern communication, which is commonplace to us, has its roots in the fantastic laboratories of determined visionaries. Sequestered in cramped, cluttered, odd rooms that often have their own appeal, science in its purest form unleashes its magic at the hands of those who study facts, dare to dream, and strive to improve. Often their pursuits are easily dismissed by narrow-minded, conservative individuals content to let things remain as they are.

The telegraph, telephone, radio, television, recording devices, satellites, and Internet all exist because of a basic need to talk and be heard in ways better than before. Once a new technology is invented, an individual or team invariably takes a step forward in the ensuing years to enhance it further for the benefit of all. The inventors, the successors, and their respective pursuits, trials, tribulations, opposition, enterprise, and accomplishments are the stuff of which legends are made and history is written.

Edward Samuel Rogers, Sr., may rightly take his place among the pantheon of communication heroes. He was a youthful and patriotic Canadian possessing the unique combination of a keen mind with a persevering spirit allied with inventive ambition, foresight, entrepreneurial drive, and marketing savvy. These elements provided him with the ability to burst forth on a thrilling, technological, ever-changing radio industry near its dawn and to grow from a youth to an adult in tandem with the growing wireless medium. He then took a bold step forward by revolutionizing radio science with the creation of a single and remarkable power tube. He extended this invention further by producing state-of-the-art receiving sets that allowed Canada to become an international leader in radio technology. Rogers went on to found a truly advanced broadcasting station that sent out programs with a level of clarity new to all. In all these ways he was able to introduce the future of communication to his own time and forever link his name to radio. An indelible mark was left upon his society, his city, his nation, and his world. The life of this radio wizard provides a tale of excitement and success that all begins with an interest, a spark, and a glance to the sky . . .

RADIO WIZARD

Family gathering with Mary Rogers (left) and her children
Elsworth, Ted and Katherine (bottom right), circa 1907

Chapter One

CHILD OF THE RADIO AGE

On the first day of summer 1900, Edward Samuel Rogers made his appearance in the world. He was the third child and youngest son born to Albert Stephen Rogers and his wife, Mary; a brother for Katherine Mary and J. Elsworth. Known as "Ted" to family and friends, the cherubic child boasted a head of thick brown curls and two large, bright blue eyes. His father was a tall, slim, serious-minded man with a thin moustache, the vice-president and general manager of the Queen City Oil Company. The young family lived at 88 Hazelton Avenue in what is now the fashionable Yorkville district of Toronto and, being religious people, practised their faith with The Society of Friends, popularly known as "Quakers."

Edward Samuel was the newest addition to a prestigious family. The Rogers roots in Canada were put down a century earlier. Timothy Rogers, Jr., came to Upper Canada in the spring of 1800 at thirty-four years of age on a lone scouting expedition. Timothy was tall and robust, originally from Lyme, New London, Connecticut, the son of Timothy Rogers, Sr., and Mercy Mary Huntley. He was a direct descendant of James Rogers, who came to Connecticut from Essex, England, in 1635 when he was only twenty years old. At the time of his death, James Rogers was the wealthiest person in the New London colony, his holdings exceeding even those of the Colonial Governor, his friend John Winthrop, Jr. At the time of his visit to Canada, Timothy was a land developer and millwright. He travelled north from the city of York through the township of Whitchurch and came across vast, uninhabited forest and he liked what he saw – potential. He promptly obtained a land grant from Lord Simcoe for eight thousand acres on Yonge Street between Aurora and Holland Landing. He returned home to Danby, Vermont, where he convinced his wife, Sarah, that the move would be good. Initially, she had little interest in leaving an established town for the Canadian wilderness. However, according to his journal, "About three weeks after, an accordance took place where my wife became willing." In February 1801, Timothy set out with twelve other Quaker families from the New England states. By April they had arrived at their new home. Timothy Rogers was the first person of European descent to settle the area, taking Lot 95, Concession 1 on the east side of Yonge Street. The following year, Timothy expanded the settlement by one thousand acres and sponsored the immigration of forty more Quakers to the community, which had become known as Newmarket because it was the "new market" outside of York for trade between newer inhabitants and Aboriginal people.

In December 1804, Timothy submitted a letter to the government:

> I, Timothy Rogers, do certify that following improvements are
> made upon the Lots hereafter mentioned –
> upon Lot 95 East side of Yonge Street – about 40 acres cleared
> – with dwelling house and other buildings

upon Lot 35 – about ten acres cleared – with Dwelling House and other buildings.

(signed)
Timothy Rogers

Lieutenant-Governor Peter Hunter agreed that Timothy had completed the requirements of his land grant, and Timothy was given ownership of the property.

Timothy Rogers introduced Quakerism to Upper Canada, founding the Yonge Street Meeting shortly after his arrival. In 1807, two acres of Rogers' land at Yonge Street and Clearmeadow Road were donated for the building of a meeting house, which opened for services in 1812. This was the first church established in the vicinity north of Toronto and later, in 1958, was one of the first sites of a provincial historical plaque. In the same year that land was provided for the Quaker church, the ambitious Timothy moved on again and purchased a mill at Dufferin's Creek, east of York along Lake Ontario. Within three years he had established the village of Pickering at this location.

Timothy was the patriarch of the Rogers family in Upper Canada, fathering some fifteen children in his lifetime. One of his great-grandsons was Samuel Rogers, one of the first of the family to establish a home in Toronto. Like his forefather, he stood tall and was stout, though he had a heavy beard and was known for wearing a carnation in the buttonhole of his suit coat. In 1881, Samuel established an oil and fuel distribution firm, Samuel Rogers and Company. It was reported that this was the first company to bring fuel into Toronto in tank cars. This organization merged with several other companies in 1896 to form the Queen City Oil Company, of which Samuel was appointed president. Queen City Oil later became the Toronto operation of Imperial Oil.

During the 1870s, Samuel and his brother Elias Rogers, Jr., were instrumental in establishing a Society of Friends in Toronto and constructing a meeting house on Berkeley Street, and later Carlton Street. In 1890, Samuel played a pivotal part in reconstructing the Religious Society of Friends after a rift that had divided the Newmarket Quaker community since 1883 and had caused the closure of Pickering College. The school was reopened in 1892, due largely to the leadership and fundraising efforts of Samuel. Samuel provided a gift to the college in 1889, funding the building of a large gymnasium, which remained standing until 1987.

In 1888, Samuel became a member of the board of trustees for the Hospital for Sick Children (HSC) in Toronto, a position he held for the remainder of his life. In September of the following year, the cornerstone was laid for a new and larger hospital co-founded by Samuel Rogers and John Ross Robertson. The HSC moved from its original eleven-room house to a new four-storey, 320-bed facility at 67 College Street, west of Bay Street, in May 1892. The Victoria Hospital for Sick Children was the first hospital in Canada exclusively for paediatrics and in ensuing years it boasted the most innovative equipment available, such as X-ray machines and the first milk-pasteurization plant in Canada. In 1930, the Nutritional Research Laboratory invented Pablum, a vitamin-enriched nutritional supplement for infants that saved thousands of lives. The role of Samuel Rogers was vital enough that the hospital hung his portrait in a place of honour at 67 College for many years afterward. In November 1993, the College Street hospital was honoured with a plaque from the Toronto Historical Board.

Albert Stephen Rogers followed in his father's footsteps, becoming a vice-president in the family firm. Albert likewise inherited his father's strong sense of community values. In December 1905, Pickering College burned to the ground. Albert quickly took the initiative and purchased vacant farmland in Newmarket, and in October 1908 the cornerstone was laid for the new Pickering College. In September 1909, Rogers House, the main academic, administrative, and residential building of the new college opened. This facility was constructed largely as a result of the personal financial assistance of Albert Rogers. Painted portraits of Samuel Rogers and his mother, Sarah Pearson Rogers, adorned the main entryway of the college. Albert christened his youngest son with a second name of Samuel in honour of his father.

When the infant Ted Rogers came into the world during that first summer of the new century, he arrived at a pivotal time in the development of radio. Advances seemed to occur almost daily, and keeping current with this exciting new science was a task in itself, reserved for only the most dedicated of enthusiasts. The astounding wonder alluded to in works of science fiction seemed to be becoming a reality. The invention promised to usher in a new age of luxury and opportunity, and to be a practical science that would develop its own industry almost overnight.

Radio was a medium dependent solely on artificial power. Without being activated by some form of electric resource, its tuner remained dormant and its speaker silent; there was no music, no commentary. To understand the principle of radio communication, one must first have an appreciation of electricity and how this science and preferred method of energy came into existence.

Electricity, by simple definition, is the motion of electrons, which causes charges. Its development, harnessing, utilization, and control occurred on an international scale because of work by men schooled in other sciences who were able to adapt their knowledge to this field for a collective benefit. The first modern scientific analysis of electricity and its properties was by English physician William Gilbert, who beginning in 1583 conducted extensive experiments and introduced the word "electric" to describe the energy force between two objects charged by friction.

A bold step forward occurred in 1672 when German physicist Otto von Guericke invented a machine that could generate electricity by means of a sulphur sphere that was rotated by turning crank – when the friction of a hand was held against it, an electric charge was produced. In 1725, British physicist Stephen Gray discovered that electric current could be conducted via hemp thread, meaning electrical energy could now be transferred from one point to another. Seven years later, French chemist Charles François de Cisternay Du Fay discovered a differentiation between two manners of electric charge, the positive and the negative. The first capacitor, a device for storing an electrical charge, came into being in 1745. Invented by Dutch physicist Pieter van Musshenbroek at the University of Leyden, the Leyden Jar consisted of a narrow-necked glass jar that contained water and was partially coated with conductive metal foil and topped with a wire rod encased in cork. The wire was then connected to a source of electricity. After contact was broken, it was found that the wire discharged a strong electric shock when placed against another conduit.

In 1800, electrochemist Count Anastasio Volta proved that when in contact with one another, dissimilar metals would create electricity. He stacked discs of copper and zinc along with cardboard that had been soaked in salt water. When he touched the top and bottom discs at the same moment, he experienced a mild shock. His Voltic Pile proved that chemical energy can be converted into dynamic electricity, that electricity can also be conducted by non-organic matter, and that a steady electric stream may be produced by the pile. He had just invented an early version of a dry-cell electric storage battery. Units of electric power measures are named "volts" in his honour.

With experiments conducted during 1819, Danish physicist and chemist Hans Christian Oersted discovered that a magnetic needle moved at right angles to a wire carrying electric current.

Thus, electricity was found to have magnetic properties, and the concept of electromagnetism was introduced. British physicist and chemist Michael Faraday expanded on this discovery and two years later was able to plot the magnetic field around an electrically active conductor. After a decade of further experimentation, he invented an induction ring and discovered electromagnetic induction, or that electric current could be generated in one wire by the electromagnetic current in another wire. Faraday's induction ring was in effect the first transformer. He later discovered a reverse principle, magneto-electric induction, which produced a steady electric current.

In 1883, Serbian American inventor and electrical engineer Nikola Tesla invented the first functional induction motor, which utilized mechanical energy from a spinning piece of iron between two stationary coils of wire to create electrical energy and a rotating magnetic field. This induced current would alternate directions as the rotor spun; thus, "alternating current" was invented and would become the most popular method of power distribution by utility companies in later years. In 1899 Tesla also discovered "terrestrial stationary waves" and proved that the earth itself could be used as a conductor and would be responsive to electrical vibrations of a certain frequency.

Thomas Alva Edison is a name that is synonymous with invention. The Wizard of Menlo Park was responsible for such important conveniences as the phonograph, an automatic telegraph repeater, the quadraplux system of transmitting four simultaneous messages, an improved stock-ticker system, the mimeograph, and the Kinetoscope – the first film projector. However, in terms of electric utility, his most notable invention was the first commercially practical incandescent light bulb, developed in 1889. This new source of artificial light was an instant and remarkable success, brightening homes and streets in a vastly improved manner over gas lamps and providing increased safety while offering a very impressive luxury. Edison made improvements on his light bulb and developed a direct current electrical distribution system complete with junction boxes, generators, light sockets, safety fuses, and conductors. He built and opened the first permanent central electric-light power plant on Pearl Street in New York City in 1882.

Thus, after some three centuries of devoted and bold experimentation, the scientific world had largely mastered an ethereal element previously thought to be the sole property of the gods of Olympus. A means by which electricity could be transmitted (wire), a method of capturing and releasing electric power (condenser) and storing electricity (battery), a power inducer (transformer), and mechanical generation (alternating current induction motor) had all been invented, studied, and improved upon. Electricity now appeared to be the order of the day, and a number of items that could be "energized" were finding themselves wired.

Yet there was more to discover, as electricity was not solely restricted to earth itself. In related work, noted American inventor Benjamin Franklin conducted extensive research tests beginning in 1746, and during June 1752 he held his famous kite experiment, wherein he wished to see if lightning would pass through metal. With a small key attached to a cord, he deliberately flew a kite during a thunderstorm. When lightning struck the kite and the key was electrified, Franklin proved that lightning was in fact a form of atmospheric electricity and actually a stream of electrified air that was identical to the electrostatic charge in a Leyden Jar.

Using the method of mathematical relations, British mathematical physicist James Clerk Maxwell further investigated the electromagnetism of Oersted and Faraday along with the properties of electromagnetic waves and light fields in 1867. He learned that the two were identical because the velocity for an electromagnetic wave and the measured velocity of light were the same. This work provided a foundation for German physicist Heinrich Rudolph Hertz, who in 1886 developed a method for producing and detecting the atmospheric electromagnetic waves of Maxwell. Hertz postulated that by manipulating electricity within electromagnetic waves, signals could be relayed at varying wavelengths. The unit of the frequency was named the hertz (Hz). These experiments and tests proved that the airwaves contained electricity and likewise that the atmosphere could transfer electric particles from one point to another.

The first step toward radio communication occurred in 1835 when American inventor Professor Samuel F. B. Morse invented an apparatus that allowed one-way communication between two points a half-mile apart through wire via electricity. British physicist Sir Charles Wheatstone and his partner British engineer Sir William Cooke invented the first electric telegraph device and successfully tested it in July 1837 when they sent and received a message along the railway line from Euston to Camden Town in England. The Needle Telegraph required five wires, each one used to manipulate one of five pointers to indicate different letters, and was initially used to control trains travelling from Euston Station to Chalk Farm in London. By 1840, the Needle Telegraph was used daily by the London and Birmingham and the Great Western railroads in Britain.

Working independently, Morse invented his version of the telegraph and successfully tested it during the autumn of 1837 in Washington, D.C. The Morse Telegraph operated on a single current controlled by a telegraph key. When pressed with a fingertip, the key completed a circuit that sent a pulse along wires. The key had a spring action that forced it back up into its "off" position once pressed. In January 1838, Morse and his partner, Alfred Vail, conducted a public demonstration with his telegraph over a ten-mile circuit at New York University and were able to transmit ten words per minute. That same year, he and Vail invented Morse code, a variable-length letter code in which tapped signals represent letters and numbers based on the principle of dots and dashes. The key is held only briefly to signify a dot, then held down three times longer to indicate a dash. The Morse Telegraph and Code was adopted internationally over the Wheatstone apparatus, along with its alphabet, as the former was easier to build and proved to be more reliable. In 1843, Morse constructed an overland telegraph line between Washington, D.C., and Baltimore, Maryland, and the next year, Vail invented the first true telegraph key, which he named the "Correspondent." On May 24, 1844, he sent the first telegram message, a Bible quote, "What Hath God Wrought!"

It was later discovered that signals could only be transmitted a distance of twenty miles before they weakened to the point where they could not be monitored. To combat this, Morse developed a telegraph relay system. There was a station with a battery-operated electromagnetic switch every twenty miles to refresh and repeat the signal and carry the message along to its appointed destination. At first, the Morse Receiver contained an electromagnetically controlled pencil that marked a scrolling paper tape to indicate a dot or a dash. In 1849, telegraphers learned to distinguish between dots and dashes just by listening, prompting the invention of a sounder to amplify telegraph sounds, and the telegraph key was modified to have a key (which boasted a curved lever) and sounder on the same base. The key was improved on again in 1881 when expert telegrapher Jesse H. Bunnell created a steel-lever telegraph key that he named the "Triumph." It was stamped from a single piece of steel and quickly became the standard tool adopted by all companies and railroads.

The year 1888 saw such a high level of telegraph traffic that operators were faced with an affliction called telegrapher's paralysis, which today is known as carpal tunnel syndrome. Bunnell dealt with this condition by creating the horizontal-action double-speed "Sideswiper." The telegraph and its modifications allowed interpersonal conversation to enter a new age, and distance, which previously caused delays and other obstacles with communication, to be bridged.

The new device quickly gained international fame. Great advances occurred over the next two decades. In 1845, the Morse Magnetic Telegraph Company was established as the first telegraph company in the United States. During that same year, a telegraph line in England transmitted the speech made by Queen Victoria at the opening of Parliament.

The first telegraph company in Canada, The Toronto, Hamilton and Niagara Electric Telegraph Company, opened in December 1846. Breakthroughs in intercontinental and international wire telegraphy were soon to follow. During the summer of 1861, the Western Union Company constructed the first extended telegraph line in the United States between St. Joseph, Missouri, and Sacramento, California. Later that year, the first transcontinental telegraph line from New York City to San Francisco began service, and by 1865, telegraph connections between Europe and India had reduced the time it took to send a message from more than a month to less than a week.

Land had been spanned by telegraph poles and wires, but what about the seas and oceans? The year 1851 brought with it the Channel Cable, which stood as the first submarine telegraph cable. It crossed the English Channel, providing a connection between England and France, specifically London and Paris. The first telegraph cable laid beneath the Atlantic Ocean was completed in August 1858, linking Ireland to Newfoundland. The first official transatlantic wire-telegraph message consisted of greetings from Queen Victoria to President James Buchanan. Transmission of the ninety-nine word message began at 10:50 AM GMT on August 16 and it was received in New York at 4:30 AM EST the following day. It was an amazing breakthrough. However, due to wear caused by the seawater, the cable deteriorated and failed after only three weeks of service. Not to be deterred, the inventors continued their work, and on July 27, 1866, the first commercially successful transatlantic telegraph cable was completed between the United Kingdom and Canada (Valentia, Ireland, to Heart's Content, New-foundland), with a land extension to the United States. Some 2,700 kilometres of sea had been bridged under the direction of John Pender and Cyrus Field, co-founders of the Anglo-American Telegraph Company. Pender and Field's Telcon cable was lighter and stronger than those previously used and was able to transmit messages at seven words per minute. The cable itself had been laid over a two-week period by the largest steamship in the world, *The Great Eastern*. Six months later, on December 20, an inaugural mes-sage was carried on the new all-Canadian telegraph system, which was officially put into operation for regular traffic. The message was sent from Westminster, British Columbia, to Canso, Nova Scotia, in three minutes, then passed on to England by the submarine cable. The wire telegraph was demonstrating that words could be sent with relative ease and speed around almost the entire world.

The telegraph was certainly a profound advancement in the history of both electronics and communication. However, having wires strung across the countryside and under the waterways pro-duced challenges, such as interference caused by weather. Some-times the wires or their supporting poles were cut or otherwise damaged. And there was the need to replace the wires or poles after ordinary wear. Wire conversation was good, to be sure, but it could be improved upon. Italian electrical engineer Guglielmo M. Marconi read about Hertz's understanding of electromagnetic waves in the atmosphere and developed a theory that he put to the test on May 10, 1894. Using a device he built that had an improved coherer (a glass tube filled with iron filings to conduct radio waves) as well as better spark oscillators, he was able to transmit a Morse S letter on a radio wave through the air via antennas situated on opposite sides of a hill three-quarters of a mile apart at Pontecchio, Italy. "Wireless" communication had just been born.

When presented with the possibility of wireless communication, the Italian government showed little interest. Early in 1896, Marconi's Irish-born mother took her son and his invention to London, where they both hoped to find more success. In early June, he filed for a patent with the government of England, and in July he demonstrated the device to a group of officials and engineers by transmitting a message between two London post offices, a mile apart. The next month, aboard a tugboat eighteen miles offshore, he was able to receive the first ship-to-shore message. The following year, the Wireless Telegraph and Signal Company Limited was founded by Marconi, and the first paid wireless messages were sent from Bournemouth, thirty-one miles across the English Channel to France.

Feeling that his wireless equipment held still more potential, Marconi travelled to Cape Race, Newfoundland, where he established a receiving station atop a hill overlooking St. John's Harbour for the firm that was then called Marconi's Wireless Telegraph Company. On December 12, 1901, Marconi fixed a receiving wire to a kite and sent it 400 feet into the air; then at 12:30 PM he received the first transatlantic wireless signal – the letter S in Morse code as sent by his employee John A. Fleming using an extremely powerful transmitter and antenna towers standing 210 feet high at the Marconi station in Poldhu, outside of Cornwall, England. A distance of 1,800 miles had been bridged by wireless communication, and the receiving point in Newfoundland was afterward known as Signal Hill. The Marconi experiment also proved that radio signals were not impeded by the curvature of the earth.

In 1902, Danish engineer Valdemar Poulsen invented the Poulsen Arc Radio Transmitter, which used an arc converter as a generator of clean and continuous wave signals. Prior to this, the spark transmitters produced strongly damped, noisy radio waves within a broad frequency spectrum. Sharp radio tuning was an impossibility as signals from nearby radio stations would invariably interfere with one another. Likewise, damped waves could not carry vocal signals. The Poulsen Arc released trains of clean waves on high frequencies, improved selectivity, eliminated dual-transmission overlapping, allowing more stations on the airwaves, increased range without increasing power, and allowed for higher telegraph speed. The Poulsen Arc was ahead of its time, but given the rate at which radio technology was developing, its usage would soon become clear and necessary.

One year almost to the day after the first transatlantic wireless signal, the first complete messages were transmitted to Poldhu from stations at Glace Bay, Nova Scotia, and the following year the first two-way transatlantic transmissions occurred between Poldhu and Cape Cod, Massachusetts. In 1907, the first transatlantic wireless service was established, operating twenty-four hours a day between Glace Bay and Clifden, Ireland. In 1905, Marconi had invented a horizontal directional aerial. In November 1911, New York City received its first wireless transmission from Marconi in Italy.

With the improved transmission of signals, steps had to be taken to improve the receivers. British electrical scientist and Marconi executive John A. Fleming extensively studied the Edison Effect, that phenomenon that describes the flow of electric current when an electrode is sealed within a vacuum tube (glass bulb) and connected to a positively charged terminal, itself an expansion of the thermionic electron tubes first tested by English physicist William Crookes in 1856, who proved that high voltage could be passed through a glass tube containing electrodes at each end.

Fleming speculated that the Edison Effect could be modified to detect oscillating radio signals. This would, in theory, vastly improve reception over the functional but delicate and erratic coherers, or the magnetic detector of Marconi, which operated better but had a tendency to have its polarity altered and thus its reception capability eliminated when placed near transmitters. After extensive experimentation, in October 1904 Fleming perfected a method utilizing a metal plate within a dual-element thermionic vacuum tube in which incoming high-frequency signals of wireless telegraphy could be rectified. This, the first diode tube, he named the Oscillation Valve, later called the Fleming Valve. Further perfection and presentation to the British scientific community occurred over the next eight months; then Fleming sent five of his valves to Marconi at Cornwall for field trials. Marconi immediately began using them, and the Marconi-Fleming Valve Receiver was produced soon after, providing better radio wave reception – just as Fleming had expected.

Dr. Lee DeForest was an American electrical engineer who sought to further enhance the Fleming Valve, which while acting as an excellent detector was limited to being a rectifier and was unresponsive to changes in signal intensity or electromagnetic radiation. He believed it was important to have a tube that could act as an amplifying detector. In October 1906, DeForest inserted a third intervening grid electrode between the cathode and anode, which strengthened the signal current as it ran through the tube. He named his invention the Audion Ampliphier. This triode tube revolutionized electronic communication and for the first time allowed a weak radio signal to be amplified as much as required, within the inherent heat limits of the tube itself. For the first time, transcontinental telephony was possible as "signal repeaters" were not required with a DeForest Audion Ampliphier. The first practical and public demonstration of the Audion came in 1910 when

DeForest broadcast a live performance of opera virtuoso Enrico Caruso from the Metropolitan Opera in New York City.

During the summer of 1912, American engineer Edwin H. Armstrong invented the Regeneration Feedback Circuit, which could increase the output of a radio transmitter and produce alternating current. Using the Audion Ampliphier, Armstrong devised a process by which part of the current at the tube plate was fed back to the grid to further strengthen incoming signals. He was able to receive distant stations so loudly that they were audible without the use of headphones, and the first radio amplifier was born. During World War I, Armstrong invented a superheterodyne circuit that used eight tubes and increased weak signals to levels previously unknown.

Meanwhile, in December 1900, radio telephony – the wireless transmission of voice – was introduced by Canadian inventor Reginald Fessenden. Previously, Fessenden had served as a chief chemist for both Edison and Westinghouse and was a professor of electrical engineering at the University of Pittsburgh. In 1898, he surmised that it was possible to use an alternator to create an electromagnetic wave that could reproduce and carry the human voice on wireless airwaves. Speaking into a carbon microphone at his laboratory on Cobb Island on the Potomac River, he sent a message to an assistant at an experimental receiver one mile away in Arlington, Virginia. "One, two, three, four. Is it snowing where you are, Mr. Thiessen? If so, telegraph back and let me know." Minutes later, Fessenden's telegraph key signalled that yes, snow was falling at Arlington. The first radio broadcast of speech was a success, and now radio carried a voice rather than coded tones.

Fessenden wished to advance the art of radio. In 1902, he commissioned General Electric to develop a high-frequency alternator, a job that was assigned to Swedish-American electrical technician Ernst F. W. Alexanderson. After two years of steady work, an alternator that would operate at high speed to produce a continuous wave at a high frequency was perfected. The Alexanderson Alternator promised to replace spark telegraph machines, which had a habit of becoming overloaded and could not offer a continual transmission. The new alternator operated at two kilowatts and was able to produce 100,000 cycles of undamped oscillations. In late 1904, an Alexanderson Alternator was delivered to Fessenden and installed in his laboratory.

At nine o'clock on Christmas Eve 1906, Fessenden conducted the first public radio broadcast from the headquarters of his National Electric Signaling Company (NESCO). Using his new invention of an alternator-transmitter combined with the principles of the 1902 Poulsen Arc Radio Transmitter and an Alexanderson Alternator, he broadcast using a 420-foot antenna tower at Blackman's Point in Brant Rock, Massachusetts, to ships in Boston Harbor and along the Atlantic seaboard. To the shock of the Marconi operators, the program consisted of a recording of Handel's "Largo" played on an Edison phonograph followed by Fessenden's own rendition of "O, Holy Night." Fessenden next read the Christmas story from the Book of Luke, then ended the program by wishing his listeners a "Merry Christmas" and requesting that they write and comment on the broadcast. The mail received confirmed that Fessenden had achieved another success. He went on to improve radio by inventing the electro-acoustic oscillator, electrolytic detector, and efficiently tuned antenna circuits. Further advances occurred within wireless telephony, and in 1916 the first North American transcontinental radio broadcast was attempted but failed due to static. January 1917 brought another test conducted between the West Coast and Hartford, Connecticut, and this time it was successful.

Wireless telephony, or "real" radio, provided even greater opportunity for the growth of the science. The Canadian House of

Commons issued the first licence in the world for an experimental radio station, named xwa, to the Marconi Wireless Telegraph Company of Canada in 1915. Test programming was conducted over the course of 1919, and the first regularly scheduled programs in the world were broadcast from Montreal's xwa in December of that year. The programs primarily comprised weather reports and the playing of gramophone records on a Victrola. In May 1921, xwa became commercially licensed as ve9am, and a year later, the call letters cfcf were assigned to the outfit. In February 1920, the Marconi Company also began a twice-daily experimental radio program, broadcasting from a 15,000-watt station built in Chelmsford, England. In June, the first advertised public broadcast concert in the world, sponsored by the *Daily Mail* newspaper of London, was made from Marconi Station 2mt Chelmsford, a recital by famous Australian soprano Dame Nellie Melba, whose singing could be heard from a thousand miles away.

In the United States, station wwj Detroit went on the air with a radio program in August. Westinghouse Electric Corporation station kdka in Pittsburgh, the first government-licensed radio station in America, began its regularly scheduled commercial broadcasting of news, sports, and music in November. During the fall of 1920, Westinghouse was the first to begin mass production of factory-made commercial radio receivers, which were produced in small wooden boxes "wired for sound" and included their own headsets, all for the retail price of $10, though the A, B, and C batteries needed to power the unit were sold separately. By the close of the year, these sets gained wide popularity, and radio was being recognized as the newest method of home entertainment. In the next few years, radio stations appeared in urban centres around the world, and receiving sets became a common sight in the parlours of many a household. Within the span of 100 years, the medium had gone from being dismissed as a "distractive toy" to becoming ensconced as a viable communication resource. At the time when radio had only recently leapt into the mainstream of society, a young Canadian boy was ready to indulge in the new interest.

BOYS WHO HAVE MADE GOOD IN AMATEUR WIRELESS

Teddy Rogers on the left hand corner, and Davy Johnston on the right, are two Rosedale experts in receiving messages. The aerial is shown in the centre on the roof of the Rogers' home, and was erected by the boys themselves. Teddy's operating room is shown below.

CITY SWEPT BY HEAVY STORM

BOATS IN DISTRESS.

Rain Fell in Torrents Down Town,
While East End Had Severe Hail-
storm—Life Savers Active.

Unheralded, and like a bolt from
the blue, came the thunderstorm that

BULGARIANS CABLE TO GREY

PROTEST AGAINST DESPATCHES.

Revolution Will Inevitably Follow the
Forcing of Greek Language and Education on the People of Other Races.

The Bulgarians living in Toronto and
district held a meeting Sunday after-

IT IS HARD ON THE SHIPPERS

WHEN CARTING TIME COMES.

Busiest Season Starts About Octoper
1, When Railways Will Cease to Con-
join With Cartage Companies.

There is apparently some apprehen-
sion on the part of the shippers and

Chapter Two

DOTS AND DASHES

Ted Rogers was introduced to wireless communication during science class at the University of Toronto Schools during the fall of 1911. The keen eleven-year-old student was instantly captivated by the concept – just think, being able to send messages almost around the world through the air by electric signals! He wanted to know more, and his interest soon developed into a hobby. Radio was in its infancy, and Ted wished to ensure he remained alongside the medium as it progressed. With some spending money provided by his parents, Ted constructed a Fessenden-type electrolytic detector device in an upstairs room at the back of the new family home at 49 Nanton Avenue in the Rosedale area of Toronto. This type of receiver was generally nicknamed a "cat whiskers" radio by those in the field because of its appearance. The set Ted created contained up-to-date spark tuning coils and condensers, and was built with the help of his older brother, Elsworth. After experimentation and development, Ted soon upgraded and built his own crystal set. However, one vital ingredient was missing: a speaker. Ted and Elsworth knew that their parents would not invest in a proper loudspeaker. While wondering what to do, one of the brothers remembered the telephone on the second floor – the one that was hardly ever used. The two mischievous boys paid a visit to that telephone and quietly removed the earpiece.

Soon afterward, they received their first signal from Station NAA in Washington, D.C. By this time, Ted and Elsworth had taught themselves Morse code and were able to translate the message. The two were so excited that they took their apparatus down to their father in the living room. To him, it was merely a jumble of strange tones, but he shared his sons' enthusiasm over the reception and was impressed when they deciphered the confused beeps into actual words. Albert Rogers was won over that day and bought his boys a proper set of radio headphones.

The following April, Ted took his crystal set with him on a family trip to their cottage at Pointe-au-Baril on Georgian Bay. One Monday morning he was listening to the device when he received some very strange messages. Could it be true? He continued to listen, wide-eyed at the news and jotting notes. He was monitoring telegraph reports about the sinking of a fantastic new luxury liner from Liverpool, England – RMS *Titanic* – as relayed by David Sarnoff from a Marconi station atop Wannamaker's Department Store in New York City. Ted wrote down the names of the survivors as well as other interesting information as it became available. Ted's crystal set was demonstrating that it had a practical use, and the fact that he was able to receive broadcasts from as far away as New York demonstrated the advanced degree of both his set and his skills.

In December, the twelve-year-old joined the newly formed Wireless Association of Toronto. This organization was made up of 104 radio enthusiasts and conducted monthly meetings. Ted was assigned the call sign XRD (- •• – •–• –••), which he used to identify himself when contacting others in the association. He prefaced and ended each message with this code designation. The association had ten rules for its members, the most stringent of which was "to interfere in no way whatever with any commercial or government station and not unduly with any other amateur station" and "to abstain from all superfluous transmitting." The following spring, Ted was assisted by his brother and Keith Russell, vice-president of the Wireless Association, in building a large radio aerial, which resembled a pyramid of fine wires, on the roof of his family home. This addition greatly increased his transmitting and receiving capabilities, but was nothing more than a large eyesore for the neighbours.

On July 21, 1913 – one month to the day after his thirteenth birthday – Ted Rogers received his first mention in a newspaper. *The Toronto Telegram* published a feature article on page 7 titled "Toronto Boys' Wireless Caught Story of Wreck in Ireland: Ten Year Old Experimenters Have Best Station in Province of Ontario – Association Is Growing – 'Teddy' Rogers and 'Davy' Johnston Are Real Marconis – Made Their Own Apparatus – Great Interest in Toronto in the Wireless Game." The story recounted how Ted monitored a message transmitted from Cape Cod, Massachusetts, about the SS *Haverford,* which ran aground among rocks off Queenstown, Ireland. Ted's set was described as "probably the very best amateur wireless apparatus in the province." The article also stated:

> Teddy Rogers is an expert operator and is filled with unbounded enthusiasm for the "wireless" game.

Albert Rogers was interviewed and said:

> I was very much amused when just a short while ago Teddy came bounding down the stairs to tell me he had received a message from Cape Cod. Of course, I had to go upstairs to hear it, and have kept it ever since.

The article included a photograph of Ted Rogers and Davy Johnston with Ted's telegraph set and the maze of wires connected to the chimney as an antenna. It bore the caption, "Boys Who Have Made Good in Amateur Wireless: Teddy Rogers, on the left hand corner, and Davy Johnston on the right, are the two Rosedale experts in receiving messages. The aerial is shown in the centre on the roof of the Rogers' home, and was erected by the boys themselves. Teddy's operating room is shown below."

Thirteen months later Ted and his telegraph set were again at the cottage on Georgian Bay. This time, while tuning in short-wave broadcasts from London, he learned of the declaration of war between England and Germany. He had the news even before the Toronto media. Ted announced it to his family, then had the information posted on the notice board at a Georgian Bay hotel.

Over the next few years Ted spent the majority of his free time working on his telegraph set and learning about innovations in the field of wireless communication. He took his apparatus with him while attending Pickering College, the school his father had built in Newmarket. In a letter home to his mother in late November 1915, Ted reported on his marks: "I came first in class again." He also mentioned that he had discovered another use for his radio equipment: "I have got a spark coil up here and have more fun than a picnic with it. Got my door knob and part of the floor electrified; make the fellows jump like everything. My room at the present time is a mass of wires."

In June 1916, he successfully completed an examination created by the Canadian Marconi Wireless Telegraph Company of Montreal and was employed by them to be an operator. Ted spent that summer, as well as the next three, serving as an operator aboard the passenger vessels that travelled up and down the Great Lakes. He would have rotated between the *Huronic*, the *Hamonic*, and the prestigious *Noronic*, all of which were owned and operated by the

Northern Navigation Company. Of the twenty-four Marconi stations situated in Ontario, Ohio, Michigan, Illinois, Wisconsin, and Minnesota, VBG Toronto, VBH Kingston, VBB Sault Ste. Marie, WDR Detroit, WGO Chicago, WME Milwaukee, and WDM Duluth were the ones Ted would have interacted with primarily. Mostly he relayed messages to and from passengers and provided news to the captain and crew. At an age when obtaining a driver's licence and perhaps having a first date are common pursuits, Ted had secured employment with the first and most prestigious radio firm in Canada. It is interesting to note that Rogers held the same position as Harold Bride, the chief Marconi operator on the *Titanic*.

In April 1919, a ban on amateur telegraphy was lifted by the Canadian government. The ban had been enacted as a war measure to keep the airwaves open for military purposes and to deter any illegal espionage transmissions. Ted had long been awaiting this day. For the price of a single dollar, he eagerly obtained one of the first amateur licences for radio telegraphy in the nation. Ted was assigned the call signal 3BP (•••– – –•• •– –•), and he began operating a half-kilowatt spark transmitter on a range of 300 metres. In 1920, Ted established a telegraph station in a small room on the ground floor of the south wing of the vacant Pickering College. From here he began broadcasting with his new signal over an aerial built in twenty-foot sections of iron pipe until it reached a height of 100 feet. Ted chose Newmarket as a broadcasting point because it provided ample space and had a high elevation. He also chose it for sentimental reasons: it was where his forebears settled on their arrival in Canada in 1801; his father had the college built in 1909; and Ted himself was an alumnus. The telegraph station became somewhat of a local attraction for Newmarket residents, who visited to see first-hand the equipment and how it operated.

At the age of nineteen, Ted Rogers enrolled in the School of Practical Science (SPS) at the University of Toronto. His intent was to formally study radio transmission and reception, to test his own theories, and to have more extensive hands-on experience with the technical side of the operation. On his application, when asked to state why he should be considered for acceptance, Ted wrote, "Have spent parts of vacations – 3 seasons – in the employ of the Canadian Marconi Wireless Telegraph Company as operator on the passenger lake boats. Have also followed the development of Radio Communication, and done some considerable experimenting in connection with same."

In July the following year, Ted successfully applied for membership in the American Radio Relay League (ARRL). This was the premier club in the world for radio enthusiasts. Based in Hartford, Connecticut, it was founded in May 1914 by Hiram Percy Maxim. The fact that Ted had been accepted once again confirmed his expertise in the medium. Three months later, he was appointed manager of Subdivision 4, Newmarket, of the newly reorganized Ontario section of the ARRL. The appointment was made by Ontario division manager Keith Russell, the person who had helped Ted construct his antenna in 1913.

In September 1921, the ARRL announced its sponsorship of the Transatlantic Test contest in QST, its official monthly magazine. Participants were advised that they would be required to send messages from their stations to a receiving point manned by ARRL executive Paul Godley in Androssan, Scotland, near Glasgow. The goal was to see if amateurs operating under certain guidelines could send a message across the Atlantic Ocean. Ted accepted the challenge and passed the stringent preliminary tests. He was assigned an exclusive marker code, NZFCO, by the league to identify himself. Ted was one of twenty-seven qualified finalists who would be participating. The basic regulations established by the ARRL specified that transmissions would be limited to wavelengths of 200 metres or less, and that the power output could not go beyond one kilowatt. On seeing these requirements, some within the wireless community dismissed the endeavour as "a ridiculous impossibility." Beginning on the evening of December 7, Ted relayed NZFCO, NZFCO repeatedly during his allotted time, from 10:15 until 10:30. He also inserted his regular call signal of 3BP to further identify himself. On December 11 he received a telegram from Hartford – 3BP had been heard! He was the first and only Canadian contestant to achieve the goal and the second most westerly person to have his signal heard, as the twenty-three others were on the Atlantic seaboard, save for one telegrapher in Cleveland, Ohio. Ted was able to send his signal from 500 miles inland. This was impressive because wireless waves travel across water much more easily than across solid earth and because he had been successful using a spark transmitter rather than a continuous wave set, whose signals are constant and typically have more power. Godley reported that the 3BP signal had been "very strong." It was the farthest that a Canadian radio unit had ever signalled, and it was done by young Ted Rogers.

Ted Rogers received newspaper attention once again with this feat. "Newmarket Wireless 'Talks' to Scotland" boldly proclaimed an article on the front page of the December 12 edition of *The Toronto Star*. Five days later, he was the subject of a more detailed story in *The Toronto Star Weekly* titled "Wireless Wizard Has Performed Big Feat: Amateur at Newmarket Establishes Transatlantic Communication – Interesting Test." The article featured a photo of Ted looking serious, dressed in a pressed white shirt, patterned tie, and suit jacket, and sporting a close-cropped haircut. To quote from the article:

> There's a young chap up in Newmarket who possesses both
> qualities of enthusiastic persistence and native talent in so
> high a degree that as a radio engineer he may some day break
> in to the class of Nikola Tesla and Alexanderson, to each of

whom can be correctly applied the expression "electrical wizard." If you ask him why he took up the study of wireless as a hobby he can't tell you exactly but thinks it was because that seemed the natural thing to do. This exploit marks him as the leader among Canadian wireless amateurs, no other of whom has been successful.

The article was reprinted in the *Newmarket Era* newspaper, without the photograph. *The Toronto Star* was enthralled enough with the telegraph skills of Ted Rogers that in September 1922 it printed a follow-up story about the event titled "Newmarket Station Heard in Scotland: Feat of Edward Rogers Last Fall Has Never Been Duplicated." This story carried a reprint of the photograph used in the December article, and stated:

> Rogers really excelled [over all of the American contestants], for while their stations were situated on the Atlantic seaboard, his is 500 miles inland. In years to come, when powerful vacuum tubes are used for the transmission of high frequency currents, it will be a source of wonder how any amateur was able to send a spark signal from Toronto to Scotland. Perhaps in time the incident will be regarded by some of the bright folks as yet unborn as a myth.

Ted was in the limelight again when his call signal was printed on the January 1922 cover of QST. So proclaims the publication:

> Transatlantic Tests Succeed!
> The Atlantic Ocean has been bridged by the signals of American amateur stations – not one but dozens of them! Paul F. Godley, sent overseas with American equipment by the ARRL, set up his station at Androssan, Scotland, and there copied the

signals of the following stations: [Listed under the SPARK category was "CAN. 3BP Newmarket, Ont".]

Within that issue, one can find the sentences, "For the first time in history the signals of United States and Canadian amateur stations have been heard across the ocean on schedule. There is but one Canadian reported, 3BP, Rogers of Newmarket, and on his spark at that from a cousin in the Dominion." *Scientific American*, long a leading publication in amateur and professional circles within the science community, had this to say in its January 1922 edition: "For the first time in the annals of amateur radio short wave low power trans Atlantic communication became a fact."

Two years after being named a winner in the Transatlantic Test, Ted Rogers made another groundbreaking achievement in amateur telegraphy. He relayed "Do you get any British amateur stations? Answer as soon as possible, BR. 2SH," a telegraph inquiry he received from telegrapher F. Hogg of London, England, to a telegraph operator in Minnesota, who passed it along to Donald Mix, Marconi operator aboard the SS *Bowdoin,* which was sailing along the Arctic Circle, captained by explorer Donald B. MacMillan of Maine. This news merited an article on the front page of the December 18 edition of *The Toronto Star* under the heading "Local Radio Fan Relays Message to MacMillan's Ship in the Arctic." Ted was interviewed and quoted for the article, stating: "I got in touch with a Minnesota operator who assured me that he would send it on, and I believe the *Bowdoin* will get it. I have already been in touch with two French amateurs and three British amateurs. I have heard them quite distinctly." Another article was titled "Amateur Establishes a New Radio Record – Successful in Holding Conversation with England." Sentences from this story bear repeating: "Early Saturday E. S. Rogers, of Toronto, succeeded in establishing what is thought to be the first amateur radio station conversation with England. The working was on 100 metres and constitutes a record for Canada and British amateur stations as far as known."

By this time Ted had matured into an adult gentleman. He was tall, standing at six feet, with most of the height in his legs – a Rogers family trait. Ted was slim and had a good sense of style, being always fashionably dressed. His thick black hair was parted on the side and combed back from a high forehead. Two piercing, bright blue eyes reflected keen intelligence. His features were of the type that turned the heads of the ladies, who gave pause at the one who was "easy on the eyes." A 1933 article appearing in *The Toronto Star Weekly* newspaper described him this way: "He is young, tall, dark, and if not handsome in the movie style, certainly good looking."

What began as a hobby for an adolescent soon developed into a full-fledged endeavour that opened doors and provided exciting opportunities for the youthful Ted Rogers. He had made a name for himself early on in amateur telegraph circles and in time was recognized as an expert. His sign, 3 BP, became familiar across North America, and Ted developed friendships with many people – some of whom he would never meet face to face. His call signal had served him well, and to celebrate this he had a special gold signet ring created, with 3 BP on its face. He had witnessed first-hand the awesome power and limitless potential offered by wireless communication and wished to enhance radio as much as possible, to make a case where the medium was appreciated and utilized by the masses rather than a select few enthusiasts. As Ted commented in the December 1921 interview, working with wireless "seemed the natural thing to do." His natural instinct was providing encouragement, rewards, media attention, and praise from his counterparts. "Rogers" and "radio" even sounded good together. The dots and dashes of Morse and the wireless waves of Marconi were mastered by young Rogers as he prepared to delve further into the field of radio.

*THE
CONSOLE*

Rogers Super A/C Console Model

Type 100—5 tube set with loud speaker
inbuilt. Equipped with 5 A/C Tubes
and Rogers Patented Power Unit.
Beautiful walnut cabinet all complete ready to plug into any light
socket.

Price $370.00

Type 105—Same without "B" Eliminator and with space for "B" Batteries.

Price $310.00

Top-of-the-line Rogers batteryless radio, 1925

Chapter Three

The Roaring Twenties…
Get a Clearer Sound

Ted Rogers stood ready to become an active player in the world of radio science, actually working on the apparatus and developing it rather than just using crystal telegraph sets. His years of wireless messaging provided him with vast first-hand knowledge, which when combined with his avid reading of technical journals and trade publications from New York City gave him what he believed to be a solid foundation for a formal entry into the field. Although successful in his classes and examinations, he remained largely dissatisfied with the radio program offered by the University of Toronto and departed the school at the close of his second year. His yearnings to further enhance his wireless skills were met with his employment as a technician at the Canadian Radio Corporation, a division of the Canadian Independent Telephone Company Limited, popularly known as CITCO, which itself was a subsidiary of the Canadian General Electric Company. It was a high point for the twenty-one-year-old Ted, as CITCO was the first and leading manufacturer of radio equipment in Toronto. In the laboratory at the corner of Wallace Avenue and Ward Street, Ted received his first practical experience in commercial radio engineering. Working under the auspices of Dr. Charles Culver, a bespectacled and scholarly man hailing from Pennsylvania who was well known within the radio and telephony circles in Canada and had been the chief high frequency engineer of CITCO since May 1920, Rogers enhanced his already fervent interest in radio and revelled in his chance to "learn from the best." And learn he did. In November 1923, as a CITCO engineer, Ted Rogers applied for his first patent after inventing an inter-stage tuned variable-coupling system. Dominion of Canada Patent 268909 was awarded to Rogers in March 1927.

In December 1923, CITCO was forced to file for bankruptcy. While to others this would have been discouraging and perhaps seemed like an end, Ted Rogers spied an opportunity. With his father he acquired the radio holdings of CITCO three months later, and from that he formed the Rogers Radio Company, whose original slogan was "Manufacturers of Radio Equipment." The administrative offices were set up in Room 405 of the Imperial Oil Building at 56 Church Street. Albert Rogers, who still served as president of Imperial Oil, was just down the hall. Ted was appointed vice-president of the new radio company. Albert, named president, managed the enterprise, and cousin Samuel Rogers, as secretary, tended to the legal issues.

This complementary father-son partnership was ideal in another way as well. Albert S. Rogers wanted his son to follow in his footsteps, and in those of his own father, to become a businessman, if not in the fuel industry at least somewhere in a managerial capacity. Ted, however, had an intense fascination with radio science and wished to pursue this as his career, to remain on the technical side of the operation. The formation of the Rogers Radio

Top: Ted Rogers as an infant,
and with his siblings Katherine and
Elsworth (right)
Above: Elsworth, Ted and Katherine
fishing with their mother, Mary, at
Pointe au Baril, Georgian Bay
Left: Rogers siblings with pike

Above: Ted Rogers and his mother at his boyhood home at 49 Nanton Avenue in the Rosedale section of Toronto

Left: Letter from home during Ted Rogers' first year at Pickering College, 1915

PICKERING COLLEGE
1842
P. C.

Jan. 28, 1915.

Dear Mother

Arrived all right. I bought some eats down in the town the other day and had a swell feed. Had a pound of sausage, jam, bread, cheese, cocoa. I have found the art of making cocoa now. It certainly was good. The sausages were fried great on the electric stove. The only trouble is is that I can't get the smell of fried sausages out of my room. I have tried by airing it

In his teen years

Opposite page: Ted Rogers aboard the family yacht, Arbie

Left: a page from one of Ted Rogers' journals recording notes of his experiments in electricity

Above: a view of his telegraph room at 103 Poplar Plains Road, circa 1922

Right: the cover page of the Rogers A/C Rectifying System patent from 1925

Top: panoramic photo of the Rogers-Majestic
Dealer Convention in July 1929 with Ted Rogers sitting front
and centre. This is the first business convention held in the newly
opened Royal York Hotel.
Left: an early advertisement for the first Rogers Radio product, 1925
Above: a window decal showing where customers can find Rogers
Batteryless Radios

Ted Rogers was an engineer for The Toronto Star *radio car, the mobile operation of* CFCA, *the first commercial radio station in the city, 1922.*

Company satisfied both interests. Albert was happy to establish Ted in a position in which he would learn to be responsible for business decisions, product manufacturing, promotion, budgets, and employees, while Ted was pleased that he could remain within his chosen profession and still have the support of his father.

Ted Rogers now had his own radio company. Enthusiasm would have run unchecked through his veins at the thought of the potential and near limitless opportunity resting at his eager fingertips. He had the skills, talent, and knowledge. But he needed a product, a means by which he could really make an improvement in radio usage. The first task he chose for himself was a monumental one. Since its inception, radio had been plagued by the problem of power supply. At that time, radios were powered by direct current (DC) A, B, and C dry-cell batteries. These were awkward to handle and quite unsightly, requiring a complicated maze of wiring between them. The sets leaked acid, which left stains on rugs, required recharging, and caused a background hum when active that caused interference when sounds were transmitted through the speaker. To make matters worse, when the B battery ran low it emitted a poignant whistling sound. The challenges posed by the batteries were what limited general acceptance of the radio as a household form of entertainment and hampered further advancement of the medium. Radio was largely an inconvenient leisure.

The primary goal of Ted Rogers was to eliminate the problems of DC batteries by finding another power source. The most obvious and most available power source was invented by Thomas Edison and Nikola Tesla between 1880 and 1883, electricity distribution. Ted knew the answer to the riddle lay within the radio tube. To quote from text written by him in 1932: "Radio tubes are, perhaps, the most vital part of radio. The discovery of tubes banished the old nerve-straining crystal set and gave us permanent, reliable radio entertainment." Developing a receiving-tube that could operate from 110-volt household electric alternating current (AC) systems would simplify everything and virtually eliminate the challenges posed by DC batteries. In a letter to his brother-in-law Jay Garner, written during the 1920s, Ted stated: "Now what we are going to make is a tube that will operate directly on alternating current house lighting current in place of the usual dry cells or storage battery and I believe it is going to be a winner as there is nothing like it at all on the market so far."

Rogers knew he would be facing formidable opposition within the radio community. Other engineers scoffed at the notion and were sceptical about AC power supply, preferring to rely on the tried-and-true batteries. "It can't be done!" Ted was told. It was supposed that using an AC current to heat the filament inside the tube would cause an ensuing hum that would not only be distracting but near-deafening and would certainly block out the broadcast signal. Given the Rogers family determination, being told it could not be done only inspired him further.

Ted Rogers embarked from Toronto in April 1924 on what would be an extensive research trip to gather knowledge for his upcoming work on the AC tube. He travelled to Pittsburgh, Pennsylvania, to visit the Westinghouse Electronics Research Laboratory, where he met American inventor Frederick S. McCullogh, who was experimenting with alternating current tubes. Rogers was shown a tray of experimental AC tubes, none of which worked. McCullogh was encountering the exact problems that other radio engineers expected – the heating filament would not operate properly. The two worked together for a short time. Foreseeing possible litigation in the future, as both were working on the same idea, Ted returned home with the Canadian rights to the experimental tube in his pocket, having purchased them from McCullogh for the princely sum of $10,000. He intended to develop it into a workable device back in Toronto.

Day after day, night after night, Ted relentlessly worked on the alternating current tube. One method was attempted, then another, and another. Each step revealed a glimmer of hope, some progress, and a step in the right direction. On August 1, 1924, success was achieved! Ted Rogers had invented an insulator for the cathode filament in Rogers Experimental Tube 15s, and this time there was no hum. The 15s boasted a five-inch height overall. The top three-quarters were enveloped in curved glass, which was enclosed and protected the minute metal workings, most prominent of which was a cylindrical filament casing and wires. The base was rounded, formed from shiny brass with four prongs jutting out from the underside. Two naked wires peered out the top of the tube, from a hole in the glass. The 15s resembled a miniature, oblong version of the space capsules made famous by the NASA Apollo missions some forty years later. The first Alternating Current Simple Rectifier Tube in the world had just been created by Ted Rogers. This innovative tube contained a better insulator that electromagnetically and electrically shielded the input and output circuits of the tube from the heater, which all but eliminated the AC hum itself. One can imagine Ted's recalling those previous comments of closed-minded skeptics. He had just proved "It *can* be done."

Ted was not one to rest on his laurels. The 15s was viable, but only part of a whole. To effectively utilize it was another matter entirely. The radio industry in Canada at that time did not exactly welcome the new modification with open arms. To use this AC tube meant retooling facilities and redesigning the receiving sets so that the new power source could be properly adapted. Battery manufacturers were less than interested because this innovation potentially spelled the end of a large part of their business. Met again with adversity, Ted Rogers persevered. During the winter of 1924–1925, he and a few trusted engineers sequestered themselves in a makeshift laboratory and set out to conduct more tests and experiments, this time with the goal of inventing a receiving set that could use the new Rogers A/C Tubes. One circuit pattern after another was tried, along with varying combinations of transformers and condensers for the internal chassis. In February 1925, while this process continued, Ted applied for a patent for his AC Rectifying System invention. Included were electrical schematics hand-drawn by him, which outlined how his invention operated. On June 16, he was awarded Patent 250174 for this system. To quote from the application: "My invention comprises producing a rectifier which may be used to supply the anode potential of thermionic (electron emitting) tubes directly from a source of alternating current of commercial frequencies such as 25 or 60 cycle without causing any disturbance in the radio reception or transmission circuits in which the tubes are used."

On April 8, 1925, history was again made. The first all-electric radio was created, operating with five Rogers A/C Tubes and the Rogers B-Eliminator Power Unit. This receiving set was later known as the Rogers Model 120. The power cord for this radio was topped with a threaded metal tab suitable for screw insertion into an electric light socket. In 1925, homes were not equipped with electric outlets, and the only reason a home had electricity was for lighting. Thus, a person would remove a light bulb and insert the radio cord. This also allowed the entire home wiring system to act as one large antenna array. Clear, clean tones spilled from the speaker when the radio was operating, and broadcasts from across continental North America could be received.

Ted Rogers' business acumen took another step forward when on May 13, 1925, with his father, Albert, and brother, Elsworth, he created the Standard Radio Manufacturing Corporation Limited. Standard Radio had the same corporate officers as Rogers Radio Limited and was the radio production arm of said company, operating from four floors measuring 30,000 square feet each at 90 Chestnut Street, Toronto, a former warehouse for the T. Eaton Company. A high level of security was established, and only guests personally authorized by Ted Rogers were permitted to enter the factory. The logo for Standard Radio Manufacturing featured an A/C Tube connected by a slim line to a triple-lamp light fixture, with the letters "S", "R", and "C" surrounding the A/C Tube.

One of the first acts of Standard Radio was to obtain ownership of all the DeForest radio patents in Canada, allowing the company access to all the radio modifications previously made by Dr. Lee DeForest in the United States since 1916. In June, Standard Radio began marketing the Rogers B-Eliminator and the Rogers Transformer. These devices contained the squat, round, light bulb – like Rogers RX-100 A/C Rectifier Tubes, and acted as adapter power conversion units, which allowed radios to operate from standard AC household electric currents rather than B-type batteries. A Rogers B-Eliminator was tested in the laboratory of *Radio* magazine by technician A. Oxley, and a report was published in their July 1925 edition that read, in part:

> The Rogers B-Eliminator submitted for test has complete and satisfactory application in all advertised functions. Special controls give perfect, smooth operating control on minimum and maximum voltages. In actual test under normal conditions, we were able to satisfactorily operate all sets tried, which included four, five, six, and seven tube sets and there was ample current and voltage at all times. A further test was made under a combination of twelve tubes and again satisfactory operation was experienced. When tested under more stringent circumstances, the results again were perfect. The current through this Eliminator is 100 per cent perfect since there is positively no hum or fluctuation to be found and this factor is the most important

consideration for successful receiver operation. We have no hesitation in recommending this Eliminator to radio users as a thoroughly reliable and valuable addition to high-class radio receiving equipment, and we look upon the introduction of this Eliminator as still further advance in the science of radio.

The B-Eliminators were offered to radio dealers on a trial basis for first-hand testing as well as demonstrations to interested customers. The first advertisement for a Rogers B-Eliminator appeared on the inside cover of the July 1925 edition of *Radio News of Canada* magazine, and a pamphlet was produced at the same time, featuring a drawing of the rectangular, wooden box-like contraption with its two tubes appearing from the top at the far end, and the amplifier and detector control knobs clearly shown at the front. The name "Rogers" was written in stylish black italic script near the top of the ad, with the words "B Eliminator" written below in a straight band design. The Eliminators retailed for $60.

This Canadian designed and manufactured instrument eliminated the need for B batteries. For some time, radio engineers had been concentrating their efforts on the application of electric-light current to radio use in the belief that the satisfactory transfer of electric-light current into radio power would be one of the most progressive steps yet made in radio development. Now, the Rogers B-Eliminator was placed on the market as the latest scientific achievement in the development of radio reception. With the Rogers B-Eliminator there was a constant source of dependable energy that greatly increased the receptive power of a set; worries about weak batteries and costly replacements were banished, and better, clearer radio reception was enjoyed. It was troubleproof and strongly built for long and steady service.

On August 26, 1925, Ted completed his modifications on the

Rogers Experimental Tube 15s, making it commercially practical and allowing it to be produced in quantity. This new tube, the Rogers Type 32, had a shiny plastic base rather than a bronze one, a circular plastic cap, and a metal "T" connecting bar to join the transformer cords to the tube, rather than the bare wire of the 15s. The name Rogers Type 32 was imprinted on the front glass.

Standard Radio began mass production of the first Rogers Batteryless Radio Receiving Set, a brand of home radio designed and engineered by Ted Rogers. It is interesting to note that the name that Ted and Standard Radio chose, "Batteryless Radio," is comparable to that of the first name for the automobile used in 1903, the "Horseless Carriage," Ted Rogers made Canada a leader in radio technology; all-electric radios were not introduced in the United States until May 1926 and in Europe not until 1927.

One console floor model and two tabletop models were available. The Type 100, the console floor model, was the crown jewel of the inaugural line, boasting a stylish design, square and elegant, complete with speaker and secured to a platform held upright by four slender legs. Type 110 was a tabletop model identical to the 100, though without the legs. Type 120, which was the first all-electric radio, constructed in April, was a rectangular model that required a separate horn speaker.

The company also sold Rogers Battery Sets with model numbers ranging from 20 to 90 for homes without electricity. The Type 130 and Type 135 were three-tube Rogers batteryless sets with sections for B-battery placement. They could be considered "half-batteryless" units, and as such were more economical. Prices for batteryless receivers ranged from $110 to $370 and for battery sets from $38.50 to $130. Cabinets for the sets were made from handsome, thick, dark walnut, which was strong and sturdy. The lid of each radio opened to expose the chassis that held the tubes, transformers, and other components. Tacked onto the inside of the lid were detailed operating instructions printed on heavy paper stock to assist the listener with his new receiver. On the far right of the sheet there were three blank columns to allow the owner to write the frequency settings, call letters, and locations of the broadcast stations that the set was able to receive. The Rogers A/C Tubes were lined up in their bolted sockets at the front of the internal chassis, which was made of black steel. They were connected via insulated wires to the B-Eliminator, which in this case was metal rather than wood, which was used in an earlier version, and rested at the rear of the chassis, boasting the rectifier tubes and the heat and voltage controls. The front of the set was dominated by polished black Bakelite plastic, which held knobs for precise station tuning. "Rogers Batteryless Super A/C" was engraved into the top centre of the faceplate.

To understand Standard Radio's position in the marketplace, it helps to consider the prices of the day. Battery sets manufactured by competitors cost between $49.50 and $170 for tabletop models, and $160 for miniature floor models. An A battery retailed for $12.98, and speakers typically were sold for between $27 and $35. A person could be the proud new owner of a Chrysler Coach motor car for $2,210, or take a lake boat cruise from Toronto to Cleveland for $13.90, or $20 if a visit to the Thousand Islands was included. The tenant of a five-bedroom apartment in a desirable neighbourhood paid a monthly rent of $80, and the annual take-home salary of a teacher was $1,000.

Standard Radio Limited rolled out its distribution on a near-national level when it secured the QRS Music Company of Canada as a representation agent for the radios in Ontario and Quebec, then the Radio Corporation of Winnipeg in Manitoba, the Canada West Electric Company in Saskatchewan and Alberta, and the Radio Corporation of Vancouver in British Columbia. Rogers Batteryless Sets were described as the "Wonder Radio," and these radios were carried by the Simpson's Department Store, which was the first retail chain to partner with Standard Radio Limited.

The QRS Music Company of Canada was created in November 1924 by brothers Frederick and Burdick (Bert) Trestrail. It was the Canadian division of the QRS of Chicago, and the firm was a progressive merchandiser, distributing radios, radio parts, phonographs, player pianos, and music rolls from their offices and showroom at 690 King Street West in Toronto. An article about the Standard Radio-QRS Canada alliance appeared in the August 1925 issue of *Radio Informer* magazine and included the statement: "This new line of radio sets, which will undoubtedly cause a furore in the trade, will be watched with great interest." This was the beginning of a long and mutually beneficial partnership between Ted Rogers and the Trestrails.

At the same time, Standard Radio introduced the logo for the Rogers Batteryless brand. It featured the word "Rogers" in large, bold ascending script, with the angled stem of the "R" joined with a loop to the sweeping curve of the "S". Written within "Rogers" was "batteryless" on a scrolling ribbon. "A/C" was written alongside, within the lower curve of the "S" in "Rogers". Beneath this was written "Radio Receiving Sets." The logo was presented as a stand-alone symbol, and was also reproduced in white within a black rectangle, bordered with a stylish design. The logo was granted Dominion of Canada Trademark 179/39693 in April 1926. Standard Radio began marketing Rogers Batteryless Radios with the slogan, "Just Plug In – Then Tune In!" It was often accompanied by a drawing of a smiling young woman, with a flashy modern bob haircut, connecting her Rogers Model 100 to a lamp socket. The "g" in "Plug" was exaggerated and redrawn to resemble a light fixture. Later slogans featured the "It CAN be Done!" phrase to emphasize the truly remarkable achievement of Ted Rogers.

The Canadian National Exhibition opened in Toronto on

August 29, providing the venue for the first public showing of Rogers Batteryless Radio Receiving Sets. Rogers radios were featured at two exhibits in this showplace of Canadian ingenuity and amusement. Standard Radio had its own display at Booth 94-A in the south wing of the Industrial Building. Previously, this booth had been used for many years by CITCO, and rights to its use reverted to Rogers after the acquisition. Rogers radios were also featured at the QRS Music Company exhibit in the Music Building. Readers of the September edition of *Radio News of Canada* magazine saw an article titled "Radio at the Canadian National Exhibition" at the front of the issue. They were advised: "The Standard Radio Company booth should be visited by all radio fans, as they have some new features that are decidedly interesting."

Standard Radio published the first advertisement for Rogers Batteryless Radio Receiving Sets in the September 3, 1925, edition of *The Toronto Star* newspaper. The large three-quarter-page advertisement featured the Rogers Batteryless logo and slogan, and drawings of the batteryless models. Rogers Batteryless Radios were also featured in a large two-page advertisement in *Radio* magazine, and Standard Radio produced its first advertising pamphlet.

As a result of the phenomenal marketing and distribution campaign in September, Rogers Batteryless Radio Receiving Sets were carried by seventeen radio and furniture dealers in Toronto during that month alone. Standard Radio went on to invite readers of *The Globe* newspaper in Toronto to listen to play-by-play live coverage of the World Series baseball game between Pittsburgh and Washington over Rogers radios at Rogers' dealers.

Of course, the success of the enterprise depended wholly on how well the new radios were received by consumers. If the public took to the idea, then the venture would be a success; however, if the sets were seen as a novelty or passing fad, then progress might be curtailed. Letters sent to Standard Radio, QRS Canada, or newspapers by thoroughly impressed customers dispelled any fears that may have lingered. The first unsolicited praise came from *The Toronto Star*. On the radio page of their August 18, 1925, edition a reporter wrote: "*The Star* was the guest of Mr. Maurice Fiegehen, 37 Grenadier Road, who, with the aid of a new 5-tube tuned radio frequency receiver, operating off the lamp socket and using no aerial or batteries, was enabled to tune in with over twenty-five stations."

The Long and Wilson Hardware Company in Walkerville, Ontario, sent a Rogers set to a radio engineer for an independent quality test, and his reply was printed in September 1925 in *The Border Cities Star* newspaper published in Windsor:

Recommends Battery-less Set

I received the Rogers A.C. Battery-less broadcast receiving set which you forwarded me for my examination and criticism. I was fully expecting sacrifice, either in the quietness of operation, or range and selectivity, had been made in order to obtain the great advantage of using house lighting service current for both "A" and "B" potentials, particularly, of twenty-five cycle frequency. I would state that the results obtained using the set, its extreme range, volume and selectivity were nothing short of a revelation to me. Under no conditions whatever is there the slightest indication of the use of alternating current on both filament and plate. If anything those potentials are more stable than that of a battery source. As to its range and volume, etc. I can only say that the claims made for this set are not in the least exaggerated. In my estimation fully 90 per cent of "radio" troubles are eliminated by excluding battery supply to the tubes, to say nothing of untidiness, corrosion of terminals, charging, and their many other disadvantages, particularly when their elimination is at absolutely no sacrifice to the receiving efficiency of the receiver.

Without hesitancy, I would recommend this apparatus to
the most exacting Radio enthusiast and feel certain that its
future demand will corroborate my conclusion in this regard.

Respectfully yours,
W. J. Carter

To quote from other letters:

STANDARD RADIO CORPORATION

Gentlemen:
Having seen your Exhibit at the Canadian National
Exhibition.... I bought a 3-Tube Rogers last November
and have had truly remarkable results with the Set up to date.
I have logged from 115 to 120 stations on Speaker, including
KFI Los Angeles, KOA Denver, WBAP Forth Worth, WOAW
Omaha, WSMB New Orleans, WSUI Iowa City, WFAA. Dallas,
WOAI San Antonio, WGHB Clearwater Fla., CFCY Charlotte-
town, three Montreal stations, etc., etc.

In addition to its D.X. qualities, tone and volume are better
than any 3-Tube of any other make that I have heard, in fact,
there are many Five's which, in my opinion, cannot compare
with your 3.

In addition the Set is so easy to tune, that on a good night
I can set the volume control at a reasonably low point, and tune
in Station after Station with one hand on the Station selector
only. The elimination of batteries, low cost of Hydro power
and long life of your wonderful A/C Tubes make the Rogers
Set a humdinger, and hard to beat at any price.

Yours very truly,
Gilbert Stagg

Mr. Frank Wood, December 9th 1925

Dear Frank:

I am very pleased with the model 120 Rogers Batteryless
Radio set which you installed in our apartments.

Mrs. Kingston and I have never cared for the ordinary type
of radio on account of the untidy wiring and fussing with the
batteries, chargers, etc. It was a revelation to us to find that the
Rogers would operate perfectly without aerial or batteries of
any kind. As a matter of fact, although I have listened to many
makes of radio sets at various times, I have never heard one that
would compare with the Rogers for tone, volume or distance
and I am thoroughly satisfied with it in every way.

Sincerely yours,
J. D. Kingston
Manager, Iroquois Hotel

A door had been opened and people could enjoy the comfort
and luxury of an impressive new world of home-use radio.
Although the actual wiring, workings, and operation remained an
elusive mystery to all but the technicians, the fact that reception
had become marginally simplified was making a great impact. Simplification without the loss of any core features, and the improvement of said features, were extra-special bonuses.

Ted Rogers was the subject of an article in the November 25
edition of *The Globe* newspaper. The piece was titled "Develops
New Type of Radio Receiver" and featured his photograph. He
gazed confidently into the camera, well dressed in a three-piece suit,
and looking surprisingly young. In part the caption stated, "He has
made many contributions to radio development, his crowning
achievement being the production of a receiving set that takes its

operating power from the alternating current of the ordinary electric light." That same month Standard Radio took an especially eye-catching full-page colour advertisement in *Maclean's* magazine.

December brought a close to an incredible year for Ted Rogers and the new Rogers Batteryless Radio, and still more media attention when Standard Radio and the Rogers Batteryless Radio were the subject of a three-page article in *Radio* magazine titled, "A Romance in Radio: Rogers Batteryless Set Creates New Standard in Radio Principles and Reception." The extensive story was accompanied by a photo of the Standard Radio building at 90 Chestnut Street; a group photo of Standard Radio executives and employees in front of the building, with Ted Rogers sitting front and centre surrounded by his partners; a photo of the administrative wing with its secretaries; and one of the radio plant with its engineers, whose caption read: "Where science and machinery meet." The last paragraph of the article was of particular merit: "Canada may well be proud of the Rogers batteryless set as an outstanding contribution to the development and simplification of radio."

Ted Rogers had made an indelible mark on the radio world. His invention of a remarkable power tube would make short work of DC batteries, and their inherent problems would soon become a thing of the past. People could now enjoy radio in ways only dreamed of before, thanks to him. His prediction to his friend Jay – "I believe it is going to be a winner as there is nothing like it at all on the market so far" – was proving true. The Rogers A/C Tube and its companion, the Rogers Batteryless Radio, were revolutionizing home entertainment and propelling Canadian audiences to a new level of sophistication. Ted proved not only that "It can be done," but that "It can be done, and done well." And he had just barely begun...

CFRB

1937

THE KEY TO CANADA'S RICHEST MARKET

YEAR BOOK
& RADIO LOG

25 CENTS

Chapter Four

ON THE AIR!

When considering his situation in the summer of 1926, Ted Rogers found himself in a highly advantageous and enviable position. Standard Radio Manufacturing stood as the exclusive provider of all electric Rogers Batteryless Radios in Canada, and the sets were being well received by dealers and consumers alike. Rogers advertisements appearing in late 1925 and early 1926 declared it would be "A Batteryless Year," and this was proving true as battery sets were beginning to be viewed as old-fashioned. The success was certainly encouraging, but the ambitious Ted wondered how he could expand further into the radio industry. The answer lay in his first love and introduction to the science, wireless broadcasting.

From the time twelve years earlier when he built his first crystal set in the attic of his parents' home, he had striven to make himself an expert in the medium. His introduction to commercial broadcasting came with his employment as a technician for CFCA, the first radio station in Toronto. Ted was instrumental in assembling station 9AH in February 1922, a facility owned and operated by *The Toronto Star* newspaper, using equipment provided by CITCO. One month later, 9AH became CFCA, the first newspaper-owned radio station in Canada, whose call letters represented Canada's First Covers America. When it began transmitting on March 28, CFCA became an early player in commercial radio in Canada. (The first Canadian broadcaster was established by the Canadian Marconi Company in the summer of 1919, station XWA in Montreal.) CFCA transmitted from studios in *The Toronto Star* building at 18 King Street West. Two eighty-foot steel towers supporting some 1,500 feet of aerials strung between them added a new dimension to the King Street skyline.

A unique innovation of CFCA was what it called "Radio on Wheels." A Ford delivery truck was converted by CITCO engineers into a travelling radio station. The only one of its type in Canada, *The Toronto Star* Radio Car was equipped with receiving equipment and a special high-powered amplifier. A three-foot wave coil antenna was encased in metal tubing that extended upward from the rear doors. A CITCO horn-style loudspeaker was mounted atop a box at the front of the vehicle above the driver's cab. Painted white with the words "Radio Station No. 1 The Toronto Star" emblazoned in black on each side, the Radio Car cruised through the city, stopping at Sunnyside Park, the Canadian National Exhibition, beaches, and anywhere else it saw crowds. Once parked, the truck would attract people as it played music over the speaker.

Ted Rogers had worked at the transmitters at 18 King Street West and had operated the Radio Car, for which Foster Hewitt was the commentator. Reporting to the chief operator, Ted was exposed to equipment substantially more advanced than his telegraph set, and during this time he worked both as a CFCA technician and a CITCO engineer —which would have been heaven on earth for him. Ted reluctantly left CFCA when he founded Rogers Radio Limited, but he departed with enhanced knowledge and a behind-the-scenes view of how a commercial radio station operated.

The Rogers Batteryless Radio was a markedly improved set; its reception capabilities and sound reproduction far exceeded other receiving sets then on the market. However, when Ted Rogers scanned the dial, he was not pleased with what was available on the airwaves. Radio stations were broadcasting what he considered to be inferior transmissions. In several cases, announcers and singers sounded as though they were speaking through glass jars, and some musical instruments produced such distorted tones over the radio that they detracted from the song itself. With the substantial financial base supplied by Standard Radio Manufacturing, Ted decided to expand further into the radio field and offer a better broadcasting alternative.

On July 13, 1926, the company won a licence from the Department of Marine and Fisheries to operate a radio broadcasting station at a frequency of 1030 kilocycles with an antenna power output of 1,000 watts and the call letters CJCQ. (The licence itself read VE9RB; "VE9" was the standard government code for transmitting licences, and "RB" was chosen by Standard Radio to signify Rogers Batteryless.) In the ensuing months, Standard Radio leased space from Tom Ryan in Ryan's Art Galleries at 515 Jarvis Street to house the studios for its new enterprise. Located in the downtown core a few blocks south of Bloor Street, the large fashionable two-storey brick mansion, which boasted an elegant entryway and its own greenhouse, had once belonged to the Massey family. The sun porch became the control room; the lounge, the main studio; the maid's room, the lobby; and the master bedroom, the station's offices. The company also acquired a lot twenty-five miles north of Toronto on the west side of Yonge Street in the south section of Aurora near Bond Lake where it built its transmitter. This area was known locally as "The Pinnacle" because it rose 1,050 feet above sea level and was surrounded by otherwise smooth countryside. On this site was built a small wooden house, which was soon filled with transmitting equipment. Two two-hundred-foot wooden masts resembling telephone poles were erected, and a single strand of copper wire was strung between them as an antenna. This outfit was soon nicknamed the "coffee pot" transmitter.

Some months later, a new voice was heard over the airwaves: "This is 9RB – testing. Sixteen minutes after midnight, Eastern Standard Time, January 29, 1927." The message had a new level of clarity and there was no static because the transmitters were being powered by a new player in commercial broadcasting – Rogers A/C Tubes. Using Rogers tubes in the transmitting end of the radio business rather than only in receiving sets gave Ted Rogers a special advantage over his competitors. The AC tubes provided more power than batteries, and this power could be utilized for transmitting with higher signal clarity as well as exceptionally crisp sound reproduction. Other 9RB tests followed as January turned into February and were received in parts of Canada and the United States that had never before received a Canadian broadcast signal. Radio editors at newspapers in Canada's major centres were bombarded with inquiries of "Who or what is 9RB?" There was no answer to this just yet, and more of a furor was created when CJCQ began its testing as well.

On February 8, Ted Rogers changed his station's call letters from CJCQ to CFRB. The new call letters represented Canada's First Rogers Batteryless. Newspaper readers on February 19 finally learned who the elusive 9RB was via a bold advertisement featuring the Rogers Batteryless logo on the radio page.

> To-night - - - at 8.45
> Tune in on the world's first Batteryless A/C
> Broadcasting Station
> (291 Metres) C-F-R-B (1000 Watts)
> with the first Batteryless A/C Set

At precisely 8:45 that Saturday evening, CFRB made its inaugural broadcast. With Jack Sharpe at the helm of the studio control room in Toronto and Edward J. Bowers manning the control board in Aurora, the switches were thrown, the tubes were aglow, and the program began: "This is CFRB, the Rogers Batteryless Radio Station in Toronto, Canada." The official opening was conducted by Attorney General W. H. Price, and Reverend W. Cameron of the Bloor Street Baptist Church, attended by Ted's sweetheart, Velma Taylor, made introductory remarks. The entire event was overseen by announcer and master of ceremonies Arthur Vandervoort. The three-hour program featured Jack Arthur conducting his Symphony Orchestra from the Uptown Theatre at Yonge and Bloor streets as well as other performers and singers. Ted Rogers was absent from the opening night gala, as he was at home listening to CFRB over his own radio to ensure that the broadcast was meeting his high standards.

CFRB provided a clearer, stronger signal and better programming than the other five radio stations then operating in Toronto, including CFCA. And CFRB was furnishing a promotion avenue for Rogers Radios. In accordance with regulations of the time, radio stations were required to identify themselves and their city of origin on the hour, every hour. When the CFRB announcers said "Canada's First Rogers Batteryless," it was all but free advertising for the Rogers Receiving Sets.

"The new station CFRB had a rousing opening, well balanced in the matter of the classical and the popular," remarked the radio editor for *The Globe* newspaper in his review the following Monday. That same day, *The Toronto Telegram* had this to say: "The new Rogers batteryless station CFRB was officially opened with an exceptionally good programme." One of the foremost trade publications also raved about CFRB. "The station marks a radical step forward in the direction of radio broadcasting stations as the Rogers

Batteryless Radio did in receiving sets. It is the first and only station to employ alternating current directly to the amplifier. A very high quality of transmission has been achieved by the use of the same 'Batteryless' principles used in Rogers' Batteryless Radio sets, with the corresponding clearness and tonal qualities that characterize these famous sets," stated *Radio News of Canada* magazine in their February 1927 edition. CFRB provided a higher definition for broadcasting thanks to the Rogers A/C Tubes.

The next month brought accolades for Rogers and CFRB. In the March 13 edition of *The New York Times*, Ted Rogers' publicity portrait was published along with a photograph of the Aurora transmitter. Beneath the photo was the caption, "Station CFRB, Canada's Latest Broadcasting Station, Twenty-five Miles North of Toronto and at an Altitude 1,050 Feet Above Sea Level. The Transmitter Is Equipped with Alternating Current Tubes Developed by E. S. Rogers, Owner of the Station, Who Has Been Prominent in Amateur Circles since 1912. It Is Said to Be the Only Station Using Vacuum Tubes Which Operate in Direct Connection with the Lighting Mains. The Wave Length Is 291 Metres."

Days later, the station received a postcard simply addressed to Rogers Battery Station, Toronto, Canada. The card, postmarked March 15, 1927, read: "Your concert 3–14–'27 was heard well by me." Signed, F. E. Seger, Honolulu, Hawaii. *The Globe* newspaper reprinted this card in April and included the statement, "Apparently Toronto's newest radio station is making itself heard almost around the girth of the world." Also, the April edition of *Radio Trade Builder* magazine published a notice about CFRB, featuring Rogers' publicity photograph.

During the summer of 1927, due to the early success of CFRB and its special connection to their community, the residents of Whitmore Township, which encompasses Aurora and Richmond Hill, renamed Sideroad 15 CFRB Sideroad. This was in recognition of the fact that the CFRB transmitter site was located northwest of the Yonge Street and Sideroad 15 intersection on The Pinnacle. It remained CFRB sideroad until 1971, when it was renamed Bloomington Sideroad after rezoning.

Ted Rogers recognized that while CFRB was primarily a vehicle for news and entertainment, he and the station also had a civic responsibility. In July 1927, CFRB rebroadcast the Dominion Day Diamond Jubilee celebrations from Ottawa. CFRB joined a network of nineteen stations from Halifax, Nova Scotia, to Victoria, British Columbia, with the key station being CNRO in Ottawa. The linking was described as "the most extensive tie-in of radio stations ever attempted in Canada and possibly the world." The celebrations marked the sixtieth anniversary of Confederation for the Dominion of Canada and included the initial peal of the carillon in the clock tower of the Parliament Buildings and speeches by the Governor General and the Prime Minister. In conjunction with this, Ted also designed the special Jubilee Edition Rogers Batteryless Radio. This set was remarkably stylish and featured imprints of a Britannia image on the knobs. With the support of Ted Rogers, the Famous Players theatres in Toronto set up Rogers Radio Model 220 sets with Rogers Symphony Speakers to carry the CFRB jubilee broadcast for their patrons. Prior to Armistice Day, Ted installed a special short-wave radio receiver at CFRB to accept a short-wave broadcast from England. CFRB transmitted an experimental rebroadcast in Toronto of a program originating 3,660 miles away in England. Ted Rogers personally supervised the broadcast on November 11 of the two-hour Armistice Memorial Service from Chelmsford, England. HRH The Prince of Wales spoke at the service, which included a choir of 10,000 people. This experiment was a resounding success, and Ted Rogers proved it was possible to conduct long-range reception and rebroadcasting.

CFRB conducted a very interesting experiment in January

1928. Ted Rogers decided to take a vacation to Europe aboard the steamship *Aquitania*. His parents were travelling through the Continent, and he wished to join them and use the opportunity to study radio conditions in various countries (it was typical of Ted to find an opportunity to conduct business while on vacation). He was aboard the vessel when it departed New York harbour on Friday, January 27. That Sunday evening found Ted not relaxing in his cabin but up in the ship's radio room. He must have been reminded of his days as a Marconi operator aboard the *Noronic* some ten years before. CFRB produced a special midnight broadcast for its founder to see if in fact it could be heard aboard a cruise liner almost halfway across the Atlantic Ocean. *The Globe* and *The Telegram* both carried stories about the impending test, *The Globe* article featuring Ted's publicity portrait with the caption "To Listen at Sea." The tests proved successful, much to the pleasure of Ted Rogers. In May of that same year, CFRB enjoyed another great achievement and a national first. The Chambers-Straits expedition to Hudson Bay reported to *The Globe* newspaper "Reception CFRB Sunday excellent." On learning this, Ted Rogers spotted an opportunity. With the company's civic responsibilities in mind, another long-range test to a ship at sea was conducted, with the station establishing a special 1,500-mile connection. CFRB was the first station in Canada to "super-broadcast" news, music, cable, and telegraph dispatches in conjunction with *The Globe* newspaper to members of the Chambers-Straits Hudson Bay Expedition in the Canadian Arctic. The Chambers personnel later replied that transmissions were received "perfectly" and that they greatly appreciated the courtesy.

The first anniversary of CFRB brought good reason to celebrate. In the year since the inaugural broadcast, the station had moved from 1030 to 640 to 570 to 960 kilocycles as Ted Rogers sought to locate the channel and antenna configuration that would permit the strongest, clearest signal. The best option seemed to be

960 so the station remained at that frequency. The power was boosted to 2,000 watts and reports of CFRB reception came from all parts of Canada and the United States, and from expedition parties in the Arctic Circle and ships sailing in the Atlantic and the Pacific. CFRB used more live talent than any other station in Canada, carrying live broadcasts during evening programming and recorded music during the day.

November 1928 was an exciting month for CFRB. Their transmitting power was increased again to 4,000 watts, and *The Globe* newspaper in Toronto began printing the "CFRB Radio Review." This weekly column provided an overview of upcoming programs broadcast over the station. Rogers Radios and CFRB joined forces to advertise in *The Globe* newspaper. In promotions for Rogers Radios one can find statements such as "Hear the Splendid Radio Programs from Station CFRB, Designed and Built by the Manufacturers of Rogers Batteryless Radios."

In February 1929, CFRB became the first station to broadcast news from the editorial room of a newspaper. A CFRB/Rogers Batteryless Remote Control Broadcasting Amplifier was installed in a small room off the main newsroom of *The Globe*. This strengthened the long-standing and beneficial relationship that had existed between CFRB and *The Globe* since the station first began broadcasting. The amplifier was designed by Ted Rogers and installed at *The Globe* offices by him, his brother, Elsworth, Jack Sharpe, and a small team of technicians. The device was wooden, long, and rectangular. It rested on a table and included a circular microphone with the CFRB call letters in a semicircle across the top. The Rogers Batteryless Radio logo adorned the left of the set, and adjacent to this was written "C.F.R.B." A small gauge was inset at the lower right. *The Globe* established an "announcing corps" and broadcast three newscasts per day. The newspaper bulletin radio service was seen as a great innovation. The practicality of it was even recognized by the federal government, and the Radio Branch of the Department of Marine and Fisheries conferred upon CFRB and *The Globe* full-time broadcasting on its own exclusive wavelength of 312 metres. In an article written by the radio editor for *The Globe* and published in the March 7, 1929, issue, it stated,

> The Globe's voice signal amplifier, used for broadcasting bulletins over CFRB, has entered its second week of work in excellent shape. The amplifier itself, as previously described, is completely operated on the Rogers A.C. principle. It is no doubt due to the smooth, even, velvety supply of power that the signals reach the broadcasting station of CFRB in such good shape.

The benefit of the radio-newspaper partnership was expertly demonstrated when a train wreck occurred at Drocourt, north of Toronto, in late March 1929. In addition to the regular afternoon news broadcasts at 12:15 and 5:20, regular programming was interrupted at one o'clock for an official statement from Canadian National Railways, providing the listening audience with almost "up to the minute" information. A candid photograph of an announcer with the amplifier was published on the radio page of the September 18 edition of *The Globe* under the caption "Caught in the Act."

The CFRB-*Globe* partnership proved particularly useful in January 1930 when the station broadcast the ballot returns of the Toronto civic election. CFRB and *The Globe* were the first on the air with the results and gave a successful election newscast. According to a *Globe* article, the alliance demonstrated "the lightning-like rapidity with which big news may be distributed when a great news organization and a powerful radio station join forces to inform people of results hot on the heels of the happenings."

March 1929 brought other important alliances for CFRB. First, the station joined the Canadian Association of Broadcasters. The CAB was formed in Toronto in January 1926 by representatives of Canadian National Railways, the Canadian Marconi Company, and the Northern Electric Company to advance the interests of privately owned commercial stations within the Dominion of Canada. Its first charter was created in June 1926 with the intent of "representing all broadcasting stations throughout the Dominion." Second, Ted Rogers travelled to New York City and negotiated an alliance with Bill Paley resulting in CFRB's joining a new radio network, the Columbia Broadcasting System (CBS), New York. An article about the alliance appeared in *The Globe* newspaper featuring Ted Rogers' publicity portrait and was entitled "Completes Big Deal." The press release as issued from New York conveyed the importance of the partnership:

Rogers Batteryless Station, CFRB, of Toronto, Canada, will join the Columbia Chain on a regular weekly basis effective Sunday evening, April 21, according to an announcement made by William S. Paley, the President of the Columbia Broadcasting System. While various Canadian broadcasters have been linked with American networks for the transmission of special events of international importance, this expansion marks the first time that a Maple Leaf station has been hooked in on a regular basis.

The Majestic Theatre of the Air broadcast by the Columbia System at 9 o'clock, Eastern standard time, every Sunday evening, will be the first weekly feature to be presented by CFRB.

The Toronto station, CFRB, is owned and operated by the Standard Radio Manufacturing Corporation, Limited and is one of the leading broadcasters in the Dominion of Canada. It has always borne the reputation of carrying only the finest of broadcasting material and consequently enjoys a large audience.

In commenting on this new expansion of the Columbia System, Mr. Paley said, "Of course, I am delighted to welcome our Canadian cousins to American radio programs, broadcast through one of their own stations."

As promised, CFRB broadcast its first CBS feature on April 21. "The Majestic Theatre of the Air," sponsored by Majestic Radios of Chicago, was the first American program to be broadcast internationally. The program, which aired for an hour beginning at nine o'clock, featured a radio-play adaptation of the film *The Alibi*. To keep the new partnership with the American network in perspective, Ted Rogers directed that prior to the Majestic Theatre program, popular Canadian soloist Redferne Hollinshead would sing "O Canada," accompanied by the Arnold Jackson Orchestra. Immediately following the program, Mr. Hollinshead sang "The Maple Leaf Forever."

Also during this month, CFRB produced a booklet about its first two broadcast years. Titled "CFRB Toronto, Station and Artists," the twenty-eight pages featured photographs and profiles of the performers heard over the station, behind-the-scenes snapshots of the studio and transmitters, as well as a three-page history of Ted Rogers and his broadcast pursuits. In September 1929, a breakthrough was made by CFRB when the federal government allowed the station to operate full time on 960 AM. Up until then, CFRB had been sharing broadcast time with other radio stations in accordance with government regulations. Now these regulations were being altered and individual frequencies assigned to stations. CFRB also conducted the first Canadian broadcast over the Rogers Batteryless Network on stations from Halifax to Calgary featuring music from the Rogers String Symphony. In October, the station broadcast the World Series from a CBS feed, and as the month closed, CFRB premiered a new performance from CBS, band music provided by Guy Lombardo and his Royal Canadians from the Hotel Roosevelt in New York City in their first live broadcast. During the latter part of 1929, Lombardo and his Royal Canadians visited Toronto and conducted a rehearsal at the CFRB studios. The Toronto audience that day was treated to four live impromptu songs by Lombardo.

CFRB was proving to be as much a success as its forerunner and counterpart, the Rogers Batteryless Radio. The station practically dominated the airwaves by providing programs with clarity and strength in a manner that made it a worthy companion to the all-electric radio. With his groundbreaking achievements in early telegraphy, the technologically amazing innovation of the Rogers A/C Tube and the Rogers Batteryless Radio, and the founding of the first all-electric radio station in the world, Ted Rogers was demonstrating electrical inventive genius like that of Edison, coupled with the broadcasting mastery of Marconi. And he had achieved all of this before reaching his thirtieth birthday.

Rogers Majestic plant, foot of Bathurst St., Toronto, circa 1929

Chapter Five

LARGEST IN THE DOMINION

Ted Rogers wanted to expand his radio operation. In October
1928, fresh on the heels of his dual success with Rogers Radios and
CFRB, Ted negotiated an alliance between Standard Radio Manufacturing and the Grigsby-Grunow Company of Chicago. Formed
earlier that year after the demise of the Grigsby, Grunow, and
Hines Company, Grigsby-Grunow was one of the largest manufacturers of radios in the United States and produced the Majestic
Electric brand of all-electric radio that operated under the slogan
"Mighty Monarch of the Air." Sales of Majestic models exceeded
those of others in the U.S. radio market owing to the superiority of
their speakers (primarily because their receiving sets boasted a large
field coil and even larger audio transformer). Rogers now operated
the Majestic trademark and exclusive Canadian manufacturing
rights for the Majestic receiving sets, and the companies combined
their engineering and production resources. On October 25,
Albert S. Rogers issued a letter announcing: "Rogers Batteryless
Radio and Majestic Electric Radio Consolidate for Canada – B. J.
Grigsby, President of Grigsby-Grunow, is named to the Board of

Directors of Standard Radio." In January 1929, this new firm took the name Rogers-Majestic Corporation. A large and exciting advertisement appearing in *The Mail and Empire* newspaper a year later featured the two logos and announced the new name to the public.

During the first official meeting of the Rogers-Majestic Corporation, the decision was made to build a new factory. A vacant lot was purchased at the northwest corner of Fleet and Bathurst streets in Toronto, and the architectural firm of Horwood and White designed a large and impressive plant. Rogers-Majestic began construction in February 1929. The building of the new facility attracted attention from the print media. "Standard Radio Corporation Erecting Large Factory" was the title of an article in *Radio Trade Builder* magazine; "New Radio Factory Going Up on Fleet Street" proclaimed *The Globe* newspaper. Both articles featured a pen-and-ink architectural drawing of the new plant, and a quote from *The Globe* piece carries merit: "The new Standard Radio Building will stand as a monument to the initiative and ability of a small group of Canadians who, early in 1925, first announced a successful light socket radio to the Canadian public. From an 'idea' to one of Canada's leading industries in four years probably establishes a new record for commercial progress."

The new plant officially opened in July that same year. The Rogers-Majestic offices and production groups relocated to their brand new $300,000 factory at 622 Fleet Street West. The two-storey plant was built from concrete and steel with several broad, high windows on each external wall for natural light and excellent ventilation. The building measured 250 feet long by 80 feet wide, with 60,000 square feet of floor space. To quote from a CFRB promotion, it contained "special automatic machinery of the most modern design for radio production." The plant included a radio-chassis assembly line, a railway-siding platform and freight-truck loading bay, driveways on both the east and west sides, a research and development office, a laboratory, a soundproof testing room, an innovative internal sprinkler system, and a spacious cafeteria. The entrance to the administrative offices was at the southeast corner of the building, while the factory entrance was at the southwest corner. Each entryway was flanked by potted plants and topped with a stone carving of the North American hemisphere that had lightning bolts emanating from it. Above this were flagpoles that hoisted the Union Jack to the sky. The plant was the largest and finest factory for radio production in Canada, and one of the best equipped in the entire world. It had been designed to accommodate 400 employees and 30 office staff, and daily output was expected to be double that of any Canadian radio factory in the past. A large white sign was situated on the north face of the building, just below the roof, bearing in black letters, "The New Home of Rogers Batteryless Radios and Majestic Electric Radios."

The Rogers–Majestic plant was located in what was called the Fleet Street Industrial Centre. Other buildings included the Loblaws warehouse, the Tip Top Tailor factory, and the Crosse and Blackwell food-processing building. The radio factory was up the street from Exhibition Park and near the Maple Leaf Baseball Stadium, home of the Toronto Maple Leaf Baseball Club.

The new facility was the subject of a detailed article in the June 26 edition of *The Globe* newspaper entitled "Rogers' New Radio Plant Is Impressive Gesture of Canadian Enterprise." In November 1929, Rogers–Majestic ran a full-page advertisement in *Radio Trade Builder* magazine. It featured an exceptional photograph of the new factory and invited people to visit the new facility while proclaiming,

Proven Performance *Built It...*
Public Preference *Keeps It Busy*
Largest Radio Plant in Canada – Most Modern
in the British Empire – Already Taxed to Capacity.

During the summer of 1930, the plant received some new decorative additions. First, the large white "New Home" sign was replaced with a long rectangular wooden sign stating "Rogers-Majestic Corp. Limited" in raised bronze against a black backdrop and flanked by the word "Radios" written in stylish script. Seven overhead lamps were positioned to shine down on the placard during the evening. Two other additions were remarkable and held national status. On the roof at the northwest side, facing westward and perpendicular to the main entrance, was erected a large neon sign proclaiming:

ROGERS AND MAJESTIC RADIOS

Three lightning bolts emanated from either side of the word "Radios." The sign was 78 feet long and 26 feet high, with the individual letters each standing 6 feet tall. It was the largest neon sign in Canada. Then, at the southeast corner of the building, a 15½-foot-tall neon sign was installed. It was in the shape of a giant radio tube, with "Rogers" displayed prominently across it on a diagonal slope. "A/C" appeared beneath it, and "Radio Tubes" below that with five prongs extending from the base. Both signs were controlled by clockwork, lighting up at dusk each evening, and they provided a bright and colourful attraction for motorists and pedestrians travelling along Fleet and Bathurst streets.

Shortly after the new factory was ready for business, Rogers-Majestic opened a 20,000-square-foot tube plant at 100 Sterling Road, near Lansdowne Road and Bloor Street, for the exclusive production and development of Rogers radio tubes. The Rogers-Majestic Corporation also announced its acquisition of the radio distribution business operated by the QRS Music Company of Canada, the first distributor of Rogers Batteryless Radios. Bert Trestrail was made vice-president of sales for Rogers-Majestic. While Rogers acquired the radio distribution, the music roll and film divisions of QRS remained with that organization. Offices for the new radio distribution department were provided in the new plant.

Albert and Ted Rogers conducted a corporate restructuring of Rogers-Majestic in March 1931. The Canadian Radio Corporation, a long-dormant company included in the acquisition of the CITCO radio holdings in 1924, was made the parent company of Rogers-Majestic, operating the brands Rogers and Majestic and managing CFRB. Ted Rogers was named president of the new firm, though he still had to answer to the chairman of the board, Albert Rogers. The CRC logo featured the words "Canadian Radio Corp. Limited" written boldly within a maple leaf. The motto "Radio Products Made in Canada" surrounded the leaf stem.

During the summer of 1932 Ted Rogers was elected to the position of president of the Rogers-Majestic Corporation. Since founding Rogers Radio Limited and Standard Radio Manufacturing in 1924 and 1925, Ted had served as vice-president while learning about the workings of the business world under the guidance and direction of his father, who acted as president. Albert Rogers retired from the presidency in August 1929 and was succeeded by renowned businessman D. H. McDougall, who boasted a long history of executive positions in the electrical and hospitality trades. Albert Rogers remained active in the company, however, assuming the role of chairman of the board. When Ted became president, McDougall was named chairman of the board, and Albert eased into a life of comfort and relaxation. At the time of Ted Rogers' election, Rogers-Majestic showed assets of $1,357,713 against liabilities of only $128,594, and the company was operating without any bank loans or mortgages.

Ted Rogers assumed his new role as company chief with characteristic vigour. One of his first undertakings was the creation of a promotional film. Titled "Canada's Finest," the twelve-minute silent film was shot during the summer of 1932. Scenes included Ted Rogers working at his desk in the Rogers-Majestic Plant, the construction of a Rogers 800 model series radio on the factory assembly line and the delivery of a completed set, the creation of a Rogers 227 Radio Tube, and a behind-the-scenes look at the CFRB studios. Text cards appeared between scenes to inform the audience of what was occurring.

In the fall, Ted Rogers and Rogers-Majestic launched a new advertising campaign in *The Daily Mail and Empire* newspaper with a feature article titled "Radio Talks." Ted personally wrote all of the pieces, which were intended to explain radio technology in a layman's terms and were printed weekly between September 19 and October 31.

RADIO TALKS
by
E. S. Rogers
President of the Rogers-Majestic Corporation – the man who made possible batteryless radio reception.

To all but a few enthusiastic amateur radio fans, the technical side of radio has been a rather confusing subject for the past eight or ten years. The public thinks far more of what a radio does than of engineering features. As long as a radio performs satisfactorily that is their only concern.

But radio today has achieved such significant engineering triumphs – has made such tremendous strides since my development of the AC Tube which made radio operation possible from the electric current in the home – that I feel many will be interested in knowing a little more about this great medium of entertainment. So let's take radio apart, in the language of the public, and see how it works.

Every Monday from this date – and for a period of six weeks – I will use this column to explain one of the many important technical features that make this year's Rogers the finest radio ever built. In explaining these I will avoid mystifying terms as far as possible.

Next Monday's issue of this paper will carry my first story on the new Rogers Tubes and what they accomplish in the seven new Rogers Radios.

In February 1934, the Canadian Radio Corporation acquired one of its principal competitors, Consolidated Industries, maker of DeForest-Crosley Radios. The DeForest Crosley Radio Corporation was created in November 1924 when Dr. Lee DeForest, inventor of the Audion Tube in 1900 and the Ultra-Audion Circuit in 1912, partnered with Powel Crosley, Jr., a leading industrialist who in 1921 developed an assembly-line system for the construction of high-quality radios at reasonable consumer cost and created the Crosley Radio Corporation. DeForest-Crosley Canada became a subsidiary of Consolidated Industries in 1932. Major J. E. Hahan, president of the DeForest Radio Corporation since 1924, and facilitator of the creation of the DeForest Radio Corporation in Canada, founded Consolidated in late 1931, a parent company manufacturing DeForest-Crosley radios, Norge Electric Refrigerators (Norge Corporation of Canada Limited was launched as a subsidiary of DeForest in February 1931), and Hammond Clocks.

Consolidated Industries had gone bankrupt prior to the acquisition by Rogers-Majestic.

The Canadian Radio Corporation was now the largest radio manufacturing organization in Canada. Ted Rogers acted as president of CRC and Rogers-Majestic, A. L. Ainsworth was named president of DeForest-Crosley Limited, and Harry Sedgewick remained president of CFRB. With the acquisition of Consolidated Industries came a manufacturing plant and warehouse at 245 Carlaw Avenue, Toronto. CRC operated from both the Rogers-Majestic Fleet Street plant and the Consolidated Industries Carlaw Avenue facility. Radio production took place at the Fleet Street plant. From this moment on, DeForest-Crosley radios produced in Canada would bear Rogers-Majestic serial numbers. CRC also began managing the Norge brand of electric refrigerators and DeForest washing machines, launched by Consolidated Industries.

Something unique in the history of Canadian radio marketing occurred during November 1933. Ted Rogers issued a full-page apology in *Radio and Electrical Sales* magazine. Demand for Rogers and Majestic radios was so high that there was a backlog of 2,751 orders for immediate delivery. In response, Rogers-Majestic increased its staff to the point where production was doubled to meet the sales requests, which were fulfilled by early December. More people were employed at the plant than ever before in Rogers radio history. It should be observed that Ted Rogers and his company were providing extra employment opportunities for Canadians at a time when Canada was struggling through the middle of the Great Depression.

Expansion happened again in late 1937 in response to consumer demand. The Canadian Radio Corporation outgrew its massive plant at 622 Fleet Street West and leased a recently vacated building at 545 Lakeshore Boulevard West, located diagonally across the street at the southeast corner of the Bathurst and

Lakeshore intersection (whose northern half is Fleet Street). The facility, an architecturally stylish building built in 1928 as a Crosse and Blackwell food products factory, was rechristened as Rogers Radio Plant Number 2. The facility provided more space for manufacturing Rogers, Majestic, and DeForest-Crosley radios.

The invention of the Rogers A/C Tube and the all-electric Rogers Batteryless Radio, and the creation of the first all-electric radio station were all extraordinary achievements and today duly hold their proper place in the history of radio. Yet, there were other important and exciting innovations to come.

In September 1928, on the third anniversary of the launch of the Rogers Batteryless Radio, Standard Radio technicians developed an Automatic Voltage Control (AVC). This maintained a uniform voltage supply to the radio tubes, regardless of the fluctuations that occurred in the electric power line. This solved the problem of voltage variations between homes, which if not properly monitored, could increase the voltage to a point where the tube was damaged and its lifespan shortened. Previously, Ted had built his Rogers Batteryless Radios with a manual voltage control and voltmeter that permitted the owner to monitor incoming power. The meter clearly showed the normal operating point, and a red stripe indicated higher voltages that could damage the tubes. The AVC was built to be simple yet strong enough to survive the rigours of shipping, and the company had declared that all Rogers Radios would carry a Rogers Automatic Voltage Control. Standard Radio had also announced that all 1929 Rogers Radios would have the feature of a plug-in jack that could be used to connect record players to the radio so that records could be heard through the Rogers Batteryless radio speaker.

The Christmas season of 1932 brought radio reception on a global scale to owners of new Rogers-Majestic receivers when the company launched an All-Wave Radio. Now listeners could have

"The whole world on a single dial." The set boasted short-wave, long-wave, and police-band reception capability, allowing people worldwide reception of foreign programs as well as domestic radio shows, and the ability to listen to exchanges between police cars and dispatchers as well as airplanes and airports and ships at sea.

Another innovation occurred when Rogers-Majestic developed the Rogers Auto Radio. The Rogers Model 918 dashboard-mounted radio receiver was introduced at the 1934 Toronto Motor Show in January. Ted Rogers secured agreements with the Ford Motor Company of Canada and General Motors Canada that Rogers-Majestic would exclusively produce auto radio sets for their new lines of cars. "Living Room Reception As You Ride" proclaimed an appealing Rogers advertisement of the day, which showed photos of Bing Crosby, Ethel Merman, and seven other popular radio stars "cruising along" with a couple in a sedan.

When Rogers-Majestic launched its 1938 line of models, they contained a spectacularly modern benefit for consumers – automatic tuning. Listeners no longer had to fine-tune a station. Instead pre-programmed stations could be received at the touch of a dial. The No-Stoop Revolving Target Tuning Dial was a large rotating metal disc with call-letter labels of ten stations. The listener put the label of the desired station to the centre position and the radio automatically tuned itself to that setting. For stations that were not listed on the dial, there was still the option of manual control. "Click! – 10 Stations in 10 Seconds – Blindfolded" stated advertisements featuring a smiling blindfolded blond woman in an evening gown tuning her radio. "The Most Revolutionary Achievement Since Batteryless Radios!" the Company proclaimed. The following year brought a further advancement of the same principle – pretuned push-button sets.

Other exciting events included Rogers' participation in the British Industries Fair of 1932. It was held in the Olympia Building in London that winter, and Rogers had the sole radio exhibit in the Canada section of the fair, which featured items exclusively produced in the British Empire. A variety of floor and table models were exhibited to English citizens as well as visitors from Continental Europe. During the fall of 1935, Rogers-Majestic published its first "Radio Log" for 1936. This fifteen-page booklet was a directory of Canadian, United States, Foreign Short-Wave, and Police radio stations. Individual broadcasters as well as the CBS and NBC networks were listed by call letters, frequency, and geographic location. Featuring an intriguing cover dominated by a globe over which was superimposed a broadcast tower with emanating rings, the logbook was described by *Radio and Electrical Sales* magazine as "probably as complete as anything of its sort that we have ever seen. And it is strictly up to date as well."

During early 1931, an advertising campaign was launched to market Rogers A/C Tubes to radio consumers. "Re-tube with ROGERS Radio Tubes" boldly proclaimed an innovative newspaper advertisement that presented the following text in the shape of a radio tube:

Canada's pioneer and finest A/C tubes
are now available for use in *any* electric radio – regardless
of make.

Put new life into your radio by putting in a set of these
famous long-life tubes.

They cost no more and are sold by all good radio dealers.

Look for the name ROGERS on the striped orange and
black carton – and accept no substitutes!

Always specify "ROGERS" when a test shows that you need
new radio tubes.

There were radio advertisements as well. Every Sunday evening at 9:30 over CFRB and twenty stations ranging nationally from Sydney, Nova Scotia, clear through to Vancouver, British Columbia, this announcement was made: "Keep your tubes at maximum efficiency. Test your tubes periodically and specify the Rogers – longest-lived of all radio tubes." The new Rogers 224+ Tube was more sensitive to receiving and amplifying radio signals than other tubes, including the original Rogers Type 32, and had the benefit of being quick heating. A minimal warm-up time meant signals could be obtained within seconds after activating the radio set.

Another accomplishment was announced in October 1933. After two years of research and development, Rogers Tubes launched the Seal-Shielded Tube. The SST used a modern full-spray shielding method that provided perfect protection against distortion and eliminated the need for tin "shielding cans," which while protecting the tubes from excessive heat, moisture, and other elements, could cause vibration in the internal radio chassis that in turn would create audio distortion. The SST was a shield and tube in one. Molten silver shielding metal was blasted onto and into the glass shell and plastic base of the radio tube in a process called "metal spraying," providing insulation and temperature control. After shielding, the tube was grey and solid, with a clear glass top and a metal tab for connection. The Rogers logo was scrolled in black across the base of the tube. Seal-Shielded Tubes were no more expensive than an ordinary tube, and were used exclusively in Rogers, Majestic, and DeForest-Crosley radios.

The following fall, Rogers Tubes renamed the Seal-Shielded Tube the Spray-Shield Tube and also marketed the Model 6H7S Mystery Tube. This innovation was described as "a development of the same engineering genius which made electric radios possible." Compared to a double-yolked egg, the Mystery Tube was an exclusively Canadian two-in-one Double Unit Tube that had twice the power of ordinary tubes, allowing stronger reception capabilities. The innovation of the Mystery Tube came in the tenth anniversary year of the invention of the Rogers A/C tube. The company later announced that all Rogers, Majestic, and DeForest-Crosley brand radios would be manufactured with the Model 6H7S Mystery Tube, as it made possible the production of the lowest-priced short- and long-wave radios on the market.

The summer of 1935 brought still another tube improvement, with the company launching the new Rogers Metal Spray Tube. It was an advancement over the Spray-Shield Tube. It had a heavier black metal coating with the Rogers logo in white on its base, a dowel guide plug, and eight prongs, making it interchangeable with other types of metal tubes. It had perfect shielding and was extremely durable. It set a higher standard in noise reduction and provided greater heat dissemination, so the set could operate at higher temperatures.

The Rogers radio station likewise developed innovations. Jack Sharpe, the head studio technician for CFRB, introduced the Combination Microphone in January 1930. It combined the condenser and carbon types of microphone in a single unit, which reduced the hazard of microphone trouble during a broadcast. One year later, CFRB introduced another useful tool, the Microphone Swing Arm. This mobile device contained a system of pulleys and allowed a radio engineer to "swing" the microphone to any area in the studio to pick up desired sounds from symphony or dance orchestras, or dramatic plays. The stationary base of the microphone stand had an extended, angled "swing arm" that could reach to any part of the studio. In January 1937, CFRB built a recording studio at its station. To quote from the CFRB 10th Anniversary Year Book, "The possibilities of this field in commercial radio are only beginning to be explored, although great strides have been made. By means of this equipment it is possible also to preserve for posterity the broadcasts of historic events so that in future years all may relive the great moments of the past." During the spring of 1930, CFRB partnered with CFCF Montreal, CNRO Ottawa, CKOC Hamilton, and CFPL London every evening to form the first regular radio network in Canada. Prompted by the success of this operation, the Canadian Radio Corporation established partnerships with radio stations across Canada and in October 1931 created the Canadian Radio Corporation Trans-Continental Network. CFRB was the flagship station of this network, which included twenty-six stations from Charlottetown, Prince Edward Island, to Vancouver, British Columbia. CFRB still retained its alliance with CBS, meaning it now had coverage across continental North America. On the tenth birthday of CFRB, Ted Rogers launched CFRX as Canada's First Rogers X-wave, the Rogers Short-Wave Station. CFRX retransmitted CFRB programs across Canada, to England, to distant parts of the United States, and to the West Indies. The station operated on 1,000 watts of power on a 49-metre band, 6.070 microcycles, and had its own antenna system, though it was co-sited with CFRB transmitters in Aurora.

CFRB was a leader in programming as well. The station introduced the first regularly scheduled sports commentary in Canada in October 1930, with reports by Wes McKnight every Monday, Wednesday, and Friday evening. McKnight, who had been the announcer in charge of remote control broadcasting for the station since 1928, covered hockey, boxing, wrestling, and horse racing, and introduced live interviews with the athletes. One year later, CFRB presented the first play-by-play Saturday night National Hockey League broadcasts live from the newly opened Maple Leaf Gardens with commentator Foster Hewitt, who had previously worked with Ted Rogers on the CFCA radio truck. CFRB remained the key hockey station for the next twelve years.

Being proactive in news and special programming was the essence of CFRB. During the fall of 1931, CFRB launched the "Beech-Nut Auction" in association with the Beech-Nut Candy Company. This fifteen-minute program was the first radio auction in Canada and was conducted daily, with the exception of Sundays. Listeners mailed in bids for items in what could be considered the first example of electronic home shopping. During the holiday season the following year, CFRB broadcast a "Christmas Greeting" from King George V live from Buckingham Palace. In the summer of 1934, Canada was enthralled by the story of five baby girls, the Dionne Quintuplets. CFRB established a remote studio with half a ton of equipment at Callander, Ontario, to provide on-site coverage on the Quints, and a series of interviews with their paediatrician, Dr. Allan Roy Dafoe. Coverage was relayed to the CBS network, which included baby-talk broadcasts by the infants themselves.

CFRB took other leadership roles as well. In November 1930 it expanded beyond Ryan's Art Galleries and relocated to the second storey of 37 Bloor Street West, at Bloor and Balmuto streets in Toronto. The new studios were opened with a lavish black-tie celebration that received extended coverage on the front page of the City Section of *The Globe* newspaper. Photos from the event graced the article, titled "CFRB Studios Opened in Grand Display." In *The Toronto Star,* a new photograph of Ted Rogers was published in an announcement of the relocation titled "Responsible for CFRB Broadcasts." Wearing a tan three-piece suit and patterned tie, Mr. Rogers stood with his body at a slight angle to the camera, yet looked directly into it, giving a full frontal view of his face.

The studios were the largest, most beautiful, best-equipped radio studios in Canada, with 2,000 feet of floor space to accommodate an audience of 1,000 and the 100-piece Rogers Versatile Symphony Orchestra. The new location featured the Gold Studio, where the majority of announcing and commentating took place; the Blue Studio, with its two pianos, ideal for smaller-scale programs; and the spacious Rose Studio, which was the largest studio in Canada, measuring fifty feet long by forty feet wide with an eighteen-foot-high ceiling. All three studios in the new facility were equipped with the Combination Microphones and Microphone Swing Arms developed by CFRB engineers in 1930 and 1931. At this time, the unique Orchestral Audition Cabinet was introduced by Jack Sharpe. This large, windowed booth on wheels allowed an orchestra conductor to listen to the music broadcast precisely as it was transmitted out of the studio while at the same time directing the musicians. Nine years later the new facilities still held prominence within the Canadian broadcasting community. In February of 1939, CFRB was described by *The Globe* newspaper as having "the most complete studio and control room in Canada with three studios and six control boards, neon lighting, and a master-clock in the control room which operates clocks throughout the studios and also flashes red warning lights at set intervals to advise performers and technicians of approaching end-times of radio programs."

CFRB was now the largest independent broadcasting station in Canada. It distributed a lavishly illustrated thirty-two-page book titled "Broadcasting: The Story of CFRB – The Rogers Batteryless Station associated with The Columbia Broadcasting System." The book reviewed the station's current facilities and activities, and the opening piece was a letter written by Ted Rogers:

> *A Message to the Radio Public*
> It has been the constant aim of the owners of the Rogers Batteryless station to keep CFRB at the forefront in radio development and progress. To accomplish our purpose, four operating years have seen four new transmitters swing into

service, each a distinct step forward in power, modulation and tonal quality. Nor is the development of CFRB confined to the transmitter alone. Each technical improvement made available in general broadcasting equipment has contributed by its addition to the continued betterment of our station. The radio public is assured that the Rogers Batteryless Station, ever abreast of the times, will serve them as only a constantly modernized broadcasting station can serve the listening audience.

Sincerely Yours,
Edward S. Rogers,
President, Canadian Radio Corporation Limited

In the months leading up to the move, Ted Rogers had designed and constructed new equipment for the transmitting plant at Aurora. These improvements boasted some ten tons of all-Canadian equipment containing a new array of tubes and transformers that constituted the most modern broadcasting equipment on the continent and provided the opportunity for better broadcast penetration and a stronger clarity of tone. With this in mind, in January 1932, CFRB applied to the Ministry of Marine and Fisheries to increase its broadcast wattage. It is interesting to note that this application was personally supported by Prime Minister R. B. Bennett. In April, the bid was approved, and CFRB boosted its transmitting power to a 10,000-watt signal, giving it twice the power of the CBC station in Toronto and the greatest coverage of any radio station in Canada. Its programs could now be heard 2,250 miles from Toronto.

Early the following year, CFRB produced a pamphlet about the new transmitting towers it was building that featured a sketch in red ink of how the new towers would appear. It was titled:

"New Wings for Words:
CFRB's New Transmission Towers Will Fling Them Farther
and Ring Them Wider"

As announced, in April 1933, the wooden CFRB broadcast masts
in Aurora were replaced by two steel antenna towers 300 feet high
and 600 feet apart, the tallest antennas in North America. They were
all-Canadian in design and construction and had a peak power of
40,000 watts. The two were dedicated by The Honourable Dr. W. G.
Martin, Minister of Public Welfare, in a special forty-five minute
program. A photograph accompanied by a detailed caption about
the new towers appeared in *The Globe* newspaper entitled "New
Towers Over Which CFRB's 10,000-Watt Signal Goes Out: 'The
Giant Voice Of The Dominion'." *The Globe* also printed an article
about the New Tower Program on the front page of its City Section, as well as a second article in the radio column titled "Old Station CFRB Sings Swan-Song; New 'RB' Glides Onto Airwaves." *The
Toronto Telegram* newspaper ran a photograph captioned with "New
CFRB Masts, Canada's Highest," and *Radio Trade Builder* magazine
also published an article about the bold new move for the station.

The quality of CFRB programming combined with its broadcast strength earned the station recognition in the United States.
The station was featured in an article appearing in a February 1936
edition of *The New York Sun* newspaper. It discussed the innovative
radio engineering at CFRB. Early the next year, CFRB was given a
special citation by *Variety*, the foremost entertainment trade publication in the United States, for being "The all around best Canadian station."

One particular incident exemplified the abilities of CFRB staff.
In the early morning hours of August 20, 1934, fire swept through
the master control room, turning the exceptional broadcasting
facilities into nothing more than blackened, melted metal. Station

Edward Samuel "Ted" Rogers, 1935

Velma M. Rogers, 1935

The Big Attack!

Target Tuning Ties Competition Price

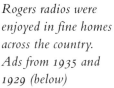

"It seems like a dream. I've never heard tone like it before."

Irresistible Avalanche of Advertising and Merchandising Material

Yes, Sir! And make no mistake—radio prospects are hearing and reading about the New-Type Rogers Radio through—

- Newspaper advertisements now appearing coast to coast.
- Broadcast messages on the air daily.
- Billboard posters confronting thousands.
- Folders—De Luxe Broadsides—Dealer Ads—Blotters—Handbills—Dealer Cut —Radio Log Books—Life-Size Display of Radio—Jumbo Cut-Out with Life-Size Model Admiring Set.
- Two Easel Cut-Out Displays for top of Radios.
- Instruction Cards for Front of Radios.

Get in on the Rogers line. Contact your nearest distributors immediately.

Entirely New Type

ROGERS
RADIO

DISTRIBUTORS
RS MAJESTIC CORPORATION LIMITED
Montreal   St. John   Winnipeg

, Limited, Calgary — Taylor and Pearson, Limited, Edmonton — H. R. Car
Regina, Saskatoon and Yorkton—Crowell Bros., Limited, Halifax.

RADIO AND ELECTRICAL SALES for September, 1935

Rogers radios were enjoyed in fine homes across the country. Ads from 1935 and 1929 (below)

*The twin 300-foot steel
CFRB broadcasting towers —
the tallest antennas in
Canada at the time, 1933*

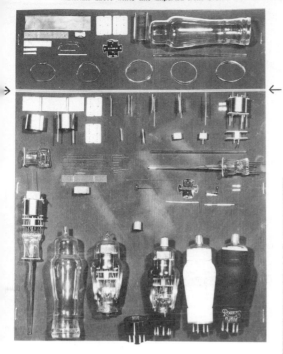

Left: An advertisement showing how a Rogers Tube was formed. It was the Rogers Alternating Current Tube which paved the way for the first all-electric radios in the world. Note the "made in Canada" pride.

Below: a giant neon sign in the shape of a tube, attached to the side of the Rogers-Majestic plant, circa 1932

Above: window display promoting Rogers A/C Tubes, 1931
Opposite page, top: CFRB *exhibit at* CNE, *1934*
Opposite page, left: unique CFRB *combination microphone, 1931*
*Opposite page, right: suggested station introductions written on
the company's original letterhead*

CFRB

Standard Radio Manufacturing Corporation Limited
90 CHESTNUT STREET   TORONTO CANADA
Telephones: Adelaide 7271-0701

Manufacturers of the Rogers "B" Eliminator.
Manufacturers of "ZOLA" Radio Sets (The Pioneer
Made in Canada)
Manufacturers of the "B" Dry-Cell Radio Sets and Acce

Sole owners of all DeForest Radio Patents in Canada.
Sole distributors for Rogers Radio, Limited, who are
manufacturers of Canadian McCullough A/C Tubes, and
owners of McCullough A/C Tube Patents for Canada.

Announcements
Studio to King Edward Hotel
Dance Orchestra

NO. 1
This is the new Rogers Batteryless station, CF
Toronto. We will leave the studio for a few
and go to the King Edward Hotel whe
dance to the music of the King Edward
dance orchestra playing in the Oak Ro
Romanelli conducting. This group will c

NO. 2
This is station CFRB at Toronto
Luigi Romanelli and his King Edward
orchestra are ready to play another group
numbers so we will return now to
of the King Edward Hotel where you wil

NU. 3
CFRB at Toronto.
We are now going back to the King
You will now hear Luigi Roman
dance orchestra play

Top right: a successful day on vacation
Top left: Ted Rogers, Sr., with Ted Rogers, Jr., 1936
Above: Ted Rogers, Jr., as a 27-year-old businessman in 1960,
tunes one of the first Rogers Batteryless Radios from 1925.

engineers, Bell Telephone technicians, and Hydro Electric experts laboured through the dawn to build a temporary control panel. CFRB began its morning schedule at 7:30 without losing a single minute, and the station maintained its seven-year record of uninterrupted broadcasts. Four days later, the master control room had been restored to its original condition.

Following a tradition established nine years before, Rogers-Majestic again operated a booth at the 1934 Canadian National Exhibition. With the inclusion of CFRB, the booth achieved another "radio first." The exhibit featured the dynamic CFRB Crystal Studio, which was a clear-glass cutaway visual broadcasting studio that displayed how a radio studio operated. It attracted enormous crowds as it actually conducted live broadcasts. The Crystal Studio was flanked by illuminated displays of the products manufactured and marketed by the Canadian Radio Corporation Limited – Rogers, Majestic, and DeForest-Crosley radios. Ted Rogers lightheartedly nicknamed the Crystal Studio "The Goldfish Bowl."

Ted Rogers also delved into matters outside of CFRB connected to broadcasting. On September 25, 1930, he was awarded one of the first licences to experiment with television in Canada. The licence issued was VE9RM; "VE9" remains the standard code given by the government for all transmitting licences, and "RM" was chosen by Ted to represent Rogers-Majestic. It was one of four television licences issued by the government and demonstrated Ted's genuine foresight. After all, television did not become a reality in Canada until 1948. Early experimentation in conjunction with the licence occurred in August 1933. CFRB personalities Foster Hewitt and Gordon Sinclair participated in a closed-circuit television projection exhibition in the Eaton's department store on College Street, Toronto. Hewitt, Sinclair, and a group of musicians worked in front of a television camera, which transmitted a picture to television sets that were standing a few feet away connected by wire.

The exhibition was conducted by CFRB in association with Western TV of Chicago and was the first public demonstration of television in Toronto, drawing large crowds of interested people. An article about the event appeared in *The Mail and Empire* newspaper. Ted and CFRB were certainly remaining current with the times, as television was first invented in England in 1929. The new medium reached the United States in July 1930 and was first demonstrated on Canadian soil in Montreal in October 1932.

In an effort to increase his position in the Canadian broadcast industry, Ted partnered with CFRB president Harry Sedgewick and friend Frank Ryan to form Western Ontario Broadcasting Limited. The company founded, owned, and operated radio station CKOK, which went on the air May 31, 1932. CKOK was one of the first radio stations in Windsor, Ontario, and on its second day of broadcasting it became a CBS affiliate station. In November 1933, CKOK merged with radio station CJGC of London, which had been operated by the *London Free Press* newspaper since its founding in 1924, and was renamed CKLW, "LW" representing London–Windsor.

The Rogers radio companies did not limit their involvement in the radio industry to manufacturing and broadcasting. Ted Rogers was active in the formation of Canadian Radio Patents Limited (CRPL) in November 1926. This consortium was made up of Standard Radio Manufacturing, the Canadian Marconi Company, the Canadian Westinghouse Company, the Canadian General Electric Company, and the Northern Electric Company. These five companies combined their collective patents and granted sublicensing privileges to each participant. Thus, a single manufacturer could have a complete patent licence to permit radio construction in Canada under the patents of all firms in the group. The CRPL charged a royalty on each radio sold by the individual members, and each year, the royalty revenues were distributed within the consortium in proportion to the value of each individual patent.

The CRPL simplified the patent situation, eliminated expensive litigation, and allowed the member companies to share technology for the overall furthering of the art of radio production. Canadian Radio Patents Limited also published notices in radio trade magazines about its patent holdings and operations. By November 1927, twelve other radio manufacturers had joined, including DeForest Radio Corporation, Stromberg-Carlson, and Canadian Brands. By June 1929, four others obtained membership, including Philco, giving CRPL a wide range of patent usage. In August 1930, Rogers-Majestic announced a plan for examining and registering radio servicemen throughout Canada. Examining and grading were expected to be done through the Radio College of Canada. By December, Rogers-Majestic allied with the Radio College of Canada to form the Radio Servicemen's Association of Canada. This association registered all competent radio men, who had to pass a practical service examination, permitting them to join the association and wear an RSA Badge.

Rogers-Majestic and CFRB proved they had a social conscience as well. Perhaps as a result of his religious upbringing as a Quaker, and certainly because of the example provided by his grandfather and father, Ted Rogers knew he had a responsibility toward his community. In September 1931, CFRB premiered "The Forum of the Air." In the interest of public service, CFRB donated broadcast time to individuals who wished to have an outlet for diverse political and social viewpoints. CFRB debuted the "University of Toronto Programs" in January 1932. This educational program was aired nightly with the exception of Sundays. Professors from the university discussed subjects ranging from Geology, History, Science and Literature to Architecture. When the Depression began to affect Canada, Rogers-Majestic and CFRB did their part to assist people. In April 1932, CFRB allied with the other Toronto radio stations for a special ninety-minute broadcast, featuring sports figures and celebrities, to assist the 50,000 Club in its Unemployment Relief Fund Campaign. During the Christmas season of 1934, the Rogers–Majestic Employees Guild selected eighty needy families in the Toronto area and provided them with gift baskets of food, clothing, and children's toys. The guild personally delivered the baskets to the families.

Ted Rogers knew that happy employees are good employees who remain loyal. Beginning in 1927, the Rogers Radio Company hosted dealer conventions in Toronto to introduce the new models of receiving sets and to thank the retailers across the country who carried their products. In January 1930, the company held a Trans-Canada Caravan with Bert Trestrail visiting major cities from Vancouver to Halifax, hosting dinners to thank local dealers and servicemen. The same month, Rogers–Majestic had employee softball, bowling, and hockey teams for both men and women. In July 1931, Ted hosted the first annual Rogers–Majestic Employee Picnic at Huttonville Park, outside of Toronto. Some 600 employees and their families attended, enjoying an afternoon of refreshments, volleyball, football, horseshoe pitching, and water sports, and an evening of dancing.

The work Ted Rogers had done within the radio field brought him recognition from the industry. In May 1927, he was elected to the Toronto chapter of the Institute of Radio Engineers (IRE) at their annual meeting. The IRE was formed in New York City in May 1912 with the merging of the Society of Wireless Telegraph Engineers, formed in Boston in 1907, and the Wireless Institute, formed in 1909 in New York. The purpose of the IRE was to advance the art and science of radio communication. The Toronto chapter was created in May 1925. The group had four levels of membership based on experience and ability. Ted was made a Member, the second-highest rank, the requirements of which were being at least twenty-five years of age, having four years of being active in radio engineering, and being recommended for membership by five other IRE members. Ted maintained his membership in the IRE for the remainder of his career. In June 1930, Ted Rogers and his executives attended the Radio Manufacturers' Association Convention and Trade Show in Atlantic City, New Jersey. With ten of its people attending, Rogers-Majestic was the best-represented company of all the firms in North America in attendance. In November of that year, Bert Trestrail gave the keynote address at a meeting of the Electric Club of Toronto. His speech was titled "The Romance of Radio," and he paid tribute to the work of Ted Rogers and the Rogers A/C Tube. Trestrail remarked that "the batteryless set was given to the radio world by a young Canadian" and continued by stating how the Rogers Batteryless Radio was the contribution of Canada to the development of radio science, and that currently the radio business stood as the sixth largest industry on the continent. In May 1933, Ted was elected as a director of the Radio Manufacturers' Association of Canada, the Canadian arm of the RMA, which was founded in June 1931. Eleven months later, Ted and Harry Sedgewick were both witnesses testifying about the impact of radio programming on the nation and the future of radio at hearings before the Canadian Radio Broadcasting Act Committee in the House of Commons, Ottawa.

During the early heyday of Rogers-Majestic and CFRB, Ted brought an end to his bachelor ways. Ted had met Velma Melissa Taylor during a social function while they were students at the University of Toronto, he studying electrical engineering while she pursued an arts program. Velma was the daughter of William J. Taylor, a prominent builder in Woodstock, Ontario. The attraction was mutual, and the courtship continued over an eight-year period, during which time Ted introduced the Rogers Batteryless Radio and launched CFRB, becoming a success with Velma alongside. On Saturday, February 1, 1930, Ted Rogers wed Velma Taylor.

They first had a marriage ceremony at the Bloor Street Baptist Church in Toronto. Then the wedding party travelled to Newmarket, where another service was performed according to the rites of the Quaker faith at the meeting house. The wedding was private and quiet, and no social notices appeared in the Toronto newspapers. The newlyweds took an extended two-month honeymoon, touring Florida, Jamaica, and Cuba. On their return to Toronto they established their first home at 12 Edmund Avenue, a large brick house in the Forest Hill area of Toronto, near the intersection of Avenue Road and St. Clair Avenue, just around the corner from the home of Ted's parents on Poplar Plains Road. Their photographs were published in the March 31 edition of *The Globe* newspaper under the caption "The Romance of Radioland." The two made quite a striking pair, he the tall, prepossessing young inventor and successful businessman with piercing blue eyes, and she standing only slightly shorter than her husband, an attractive woman with an elegant sense of style and copper hair curled close to her head in the fashion of the day. On May 27, 1933, the couple became a family with the birth of a son, Edward S. "Ted" Rogers, Jr., named after his father. The healthy, round-faced baby boy was welcomed by his loving parents and in the coming months was baptized as a Baptist. In May 1934, Ted Rogers moved his wife and year-old son into a stately stone house at 405 Glen Ayr Road, situated north of Forest Hill Village. While young Ted was cared for and Velma established their home, Ted Sr. was quick to build a radio laboratory in the basement for his communications experiments.

Ted received recognition from his community as well. He merited an entry in the prestigious *Who's Who in Canada 1928-29: An Illustrated Biographic Record of Men and Women of the Time*. This was quite remarkable for a twenty-seven-year-old. He joined his great-grandfather Elias, his father's cousin Alfred, and his father, Albert, who collectively made their first appearance in the 1917 edition.

Ted's entry read as follows:

Edward Samuel Rogers

ROGERS, Edward Samuel —Vice-President, Standard Radio
Manufacturing Limited (established 1924), 90 Chestnut St.,
Toronto Ontario; Vice-President, Rogers Radio Tubes Ltd.
Born Toronto, June 21, 1900, son of Albert S. and Mary;
School, Toronto; University of Toronto. After (Elsworth)
Rogers. Educated: University; Leaving the University, joined
the Independent Telephone Company as an Engineer, 1922;
gave considerable time to experimental work and formed the
companies of Standard Radio Manufacturing Corporation,
Ltd. and the Rogers Radio Tubes, Ltd., 1924–25 assuming the
position of Vice-President, which he still holds. Clubs:
R.C.Y.C.; Granite; Recreations: Yachting, riding, motoring.
Religious Society of Friends. Residence: 103 Poplar Plains
Road, Toronto, Ontario.

In the fall of 1934, Ted and Velma Rogers achieved the ultimate
in social standing when they made their first appearance in *The
Torontonian Society Blue Book and Club Membership Register: The
Social Register for the 1934–35 Season.* Ted was listed as being a member in good standing of the Granite Club, the Royal Canadian
Yacht Club and the York Downs Golf Club, while his wife enjoyed
membership in the Ladies' Golf and Tennis Club.

Ted was the recipient of great acclaim from the Toronto newspapers as well. In 1933, *The Toronto Telegram* newspaper began a special column that analyzed the signatures of prominent people. The
May 11 entry of "Character from Handwriting" profiled that of
Ted in the form of his proper name, Edward S. Rogers:

The outstanding characteristic of this signature is imagination of the special sort that not only foresees but is capable of creating opportunity. This man has an inventive and resourceful type of mind. He is self confident, self reliant, and seeks responsibility. At the same time and along with the evidence of strong practicality and marked executive ability there are just as strong and just as marked evidence of dreaminess, idealism, high degree of sensitivity and humanitarian sympathy. On the one hand, the ambition, the intrepidity, the powers of mature manhood. On the other, the aspirations, the reckless championship of humanity and of causes, the aestheticism and the graces – attributes of ideal youth. On either hand – seriousness of purpose, dignity, strong reserve.

In February 1934, *The Globe* newspaper published a special twenty-four-page section titled "Builders of Greater Toronto" that recognized the contributions to the city made by prominent Toronto citizens. A photograph of Ted in a serious pose with the caption "Edward S. Rogers, President, Rogers-Majestic Corp." appeared on page six of the section, ranking him number 144 out of the 792 people profiled. He also had the distinction of being one of the younger businessmen featured.

Ted Rogers and Rogers-Majestic were the subject of an astounding seven-page special feature article in *The Globe* newspaper. The piece led with a large print of the current publicity photograph of Ted under the caption "The Man Whose Genius Created Batteryless Radio." The article profiled the Rogers-Majestic Plant as well as key executives. Of particular importance, Ted was asked to write the lead story. It was the first time he wrote for a newspaper, and the piece truly reflected his intellect and ability with words:

Better and Better Broadcasting
Assures Radio of Greater Future;
While New Receivers Keep Pace

———

E. S. Rogers Tells Why
Radio Must Continue to Go Forward

It is to be expected that a manufacturer would predict a bright future for his particular product. But when I say that I believe there is an era of even greater things in the future for the radio business, I base that statement on something more than a selfish belief in our own product.

REASON FOR CONFIDENCE

That one factor makes me so confident of the future is broadcasting. Broadcasting is going on, and on, and on. We have only started to know anything about broadcasting and the part that it can be made to play in our daily lives.

As long as broadcasting continues to improve at the rate that it has in the past, radio has a great outlook before it. The radio receiving set itself has taken wonderful strides. Constantly nearer perfection in its performance, constantly smoother and more powerful in operation, constantly improving in tone, the modern radio receiving set is efficient and satisfactory to a very high degree.

THE FORCE BEHIND

And back of it all is this great force known as broadcasting. How many radio owners, listening to a program in the comfort of their own homes, stop to consider the hours of preparation and rehearsal that preceded the actual radio broadcast? The good radio program is as carefully conceived and rehearsed as many a play.

No Middle Course

The studio director or the man who "buys time" on the air realizes that he has an opportunity of attracting thousands of listeners to his program, or of turning them away. The first impression that his broadcast makes on the listener determines whether he is to be given a hearing or whether he will be shut off. With radio there is no middle course, the receiving set either reproduces his program, or is wholly closed to his program. On the newspaper page his advertisement may not be read, but it does have the opportunity of leaving a certain impression on the minds of the newspaper readers. Not so with radio. His audience, broadly speaking, gets his message in full, or does not get it at all. A good radio broadcast quickly wins its reward. It gains steady listeners just as a serial story gains interested and steady readers.

When it comes to the art of broadcasting, the art of entertaining over the air, I feel that we are all in our infancy. Greater things are before us. That is why I say radio has a future that none of us can fathom.

Greatest Unifier

Here, we in Canada are on the eve of a nationwide election and radio is playing a major part in moulding the opinions of people. Radio, through chain hook-up, gives the man or woman in the Maritimes an opportunity to think the same thoughts that are in the mind of the man in British Columbia. Radio is the greatest force ever known for unifying a nation and a people.

Radio is the greatest peace emissary the world has ever

known. Radio does more to bring about an understanding between nations than any other source. Consider the very close contact and understanding between the people of Canada and the United States brought about through the interchange of radio programs. Just as American programs reach the ears of Canadian listeners, so do broadcasts originating in Canada reach the ears of our neighbours on the south. Chain hook-ups having their origin in Canada are carried by a similar system of chain stations to every nook and corner of the United States.

GREATER THINGS IN STORE

In the advancement of science, education, religion, entertainment, the spreading of news, in politics, the world has so far seen only a fraction of what is in store for radio owners now and in the future.

Ted Rogers and his radio history were also thoroughly discussed in an article printed in *The Toronto Star Weekly* newspaper titled "From a Hobby to a Big Business" in April 1933. This was especially noteworthy as *The Toronto Star* typically wrote stories almost exclusively about its own station, CFCA. The fact that it ventured beyond its "in-house broadcaster" indicated the interest in and prominence of Ted Rogers and his broadcasting endeavours. In July the following year, Ted was again the subject of a half-page feature article, this time in *The Toronto Evening Telegram*. His radio achievements were reviewed in detail, but what made this piece more interesting was that Ted was interviewed and commented on the possibility of television broadcasting. "What we shall see will be a lofty tower in Toronto, for instance, with an operator flashing out the spectacle of hockey games, prize fights, wrestling matches, political meetings, or other such entertainment for the multitude, while people look on with their home apparatus."

Ted Rogers found himself president of the largest radio manufacturing operation in Canada and operating the largest and most
powerful broadcasting station in the nation. His receiving sets were
in homes across the country, and his radio programs could be heard
from coast to coast. He was one of the youngest industrial leaders
in a key business centre, and somewhat of a media personality,
though quite a reluctant celebrity. He owned a large house in the
most fashionable area of Toronto, drove a shiny Packard, and captained an impressive custom-made yacht. Yet, more importantly, he
was a family man with a beautiful and loving wife by his side, and
an heir to his name – both of whom he cherished. He was, by all
accounts, a genuine success. Ted was also a person in whom many
people took a great deal of pride. A son, a brother, a husband, a
father, a friend, an inventor, a broadcaster, a businessman, an
employer, a personality, a national communications hero – these
were the varied roles of Ted Rogers. Although he enjoyed a life of
privilege, he faced and overcame many trials and tribulations and
worked long, hard hours either in his laboratory or at the negotia-
tion table to earn everything he achieved. Once one of his many
undertakings was accomplished, he did not bask in the glory but
sought out the next opportunity, and on finding it, grasped it with
characteristic zeal. Ted was a man of character and of values – a
role model with an easy smile and calm manner who made time
for many a person who wished to speak with him. Ted Rogers was
a rare breed of man, and a champion of his time.

Canadian Radio Corporation Limited

WINNIPEG ·· MONTREAL

TORONTO 2, CANADA

ADDRESS ALL COMMUNICATIONS TO THE
CORPORATION — NOT TO INDIVIDUALS.

MAIN PLANT

PLANT NO. 2

May 10, 1939.

IN MEMORIAM

Our beloved "Ted" Rogers is gone.

Just 14 years, almost to the month, after he had perfected and introduced the world's first successful Batteryless Radio, which revolutionized radio reception, young "Ted" Rogers passed away during the night of Friday, May 5, 1939, at the Toronto General Hospital, after only 48 hours of illness.

Only about a month away from his 39th birthday his end came suddenly, unexpected and dramatic. Active and in good spirits, he spent an exceedingly busy day on Wednesday and Wednesday evening, May 3rd.

During the night he suffered his first attack and was removed to the hospital, where despite an operation, blood transfusions and every possible effort, he died after 48 hours, but not before putting up a characteristically stubborn and gallant fight. From an apparently hopeless condition Thursday night he rallied and late Friday was given a fighting chance to survive when suddenly, sadly weakened after a vain struggle, he passed away.

In our organization are a score or more of boys and girls today who have been associated with "Ted" almost continuously ever since the start of the Rogers Batteryless Radio, when, in a world of doubt, dire prophecies and misgivings, he formed the foundation of what eventually developed into the largest organization of its kind in Canada.

Also associated with us today are another score or more of employees who, during those early days of pioneer development, formed the backbone of the keenest competition we then had--DeForest Crosley.

To all of these old associates, as well as to the hundreds of newer ones and, of course, to the jobbers, dealers, and their salesmen and servicemen, "Ted" will always be remembered as a shy, modest and unassuming young genius, who, at our conventions or meetings, could barely be persuaded to rise and accept, with a bow, the tribute of his admirers.

Developing in recent years into a tall, robust, young man, with many responsibilities and activities, he still remained a boy at heart and

Chapter Six

REQUIEM FOR A GENIUS

Wednesday, May 3, 1939, was what has been described as an exceedingly busy day for Ted Rogers. After managing a hectic schedule and completing his work, he left his office and travelled north up Spadina Road in his white Packard automobile as dusk was falling. He patiently manoeuvred through rush hour traffic along streets still slick from an earlier rainstorm, with thoughts of the next day's tasks no doubt racing through his mind. On reaching his home, he, Velma, and Ted, Jr., entertained dinner guests. Ted, Jr., was then put to bed, Velma retired to read, and Ted went to his makeshift radio laboratory in the basement to conduct experiments – his preferred method of unwinding after a long day at the plant.

During the late evening, Velma was suddenly wakened by the sounds of a sputtering cough and unintelligible moans. She saw that Ted was no longer in bed and noticed light coming from the master bathroom, whose door was slightly ajar. Calling out for her husband, she approached, but received no reply. Velma rested her hand on the door and opened it gently. Ted was hunched over the sink, seemingly unconscious. Heavy droplets of crimson stained the wallpaper, and there was evidence he had been bleeding from the corner of his mouth.

An ambulance arrived at 405 Glen Ayr Road, and Ted was quickly taken to Toronto General Hospital, where the diagnosis revealed a combination that would have easily felled a weaker man. An ulcer caused by extreme stress from overwork hemorrhaged at the same time that an aneurysm erupted. Surgeons performed an emergency operation, blood transfusions were given, and medicines were administered. Ted was settled in a room in the Private Patients Pavilion to sleep and recover. The prognosis looked good late on Friday afternoon as he appeared to rally. The unexpected struck once again when a second attack occurred, and he passed away early Saturday morning, May 6, 1939, at the age of thirty-eight.

It was a tremendous shock to his family, to the Toronto business community, to his admirers, and to the radio industry in general. Morning editions of the Toronto newspapers carried the story. "Gave World Light-Radio, Edward Rogers, 38, Dies" stated the headline of an extended article in *The Toronto Star*. To quote from the article, which reviewed the high points of his life:

> Ted Rogers found that music came through his light socket tube sweetly and clearly. Exactly one year after he brought back the "hopeless" tube from the United States, he placed on the world market the first commercial light socket radio receiving set. That was in 1925. It was this set that led to wide-spread use of the present day batteryless sets now in universal use. It has been said that Canada's great radio station CFRB can be called 3BP enlarged because it was from that station through which Ted Rogers could talk to many of his fellow experimenters in the realm of radio.

To quote from *The Toronto Telegram:*

> Edward Samuel Rogers discovered for the world the principle
> by which home radios could be operated electronically. In
> 1925, Ted Rogers marketed the first electric radio the world
> had ever known. About that discovery was founded the
> Rogers-Majestic Corporation of which he was president at
> his death, and from his early station, 3 BP, grew Canada's most
> powerful private radio station, CFRB, which he also headed. His
> death is a deep blow to Canadian radio circles. Since its infancy
> he had worked for the good of Canadian radio, made for
> himself thousands of friends in the industry and outside it. He
> was one of the youngest of Canada's business leaders.

And from *The Globe:*

> Edward Samuel Rogers gave the world his electric radio
> receiver before he had reached his middle twenties. He was a
> young man who declined to let obstacles stand in the way of
> success. His invention conferred great blessings on mankind.
> Like the inventor of the telephone and electric light, Ted
> Rogers often "burned the midnight oil" before he worked out
> the problem which had baffled older heads. He spent long
> hours in laboratories and worked his tiny transmitter at night,
> sending signals across the seas. Young folks and old were thrilled
> by his success. It provides a lesson for other young men inclined
> to the defeatist attitude.

Variety had this headline in the international radio section of its
May 10 edition, "Canadian Pioneer Dies at 38: Ted Rogers, Manufacturer and Operator of CFRB Toronto Had Spectacular Success."

The funeral occurred on May 8 at the family home. Friends,

dignitaries, colleagues, and business associates, including executives from various radio networks in the United States, assembled to pay their final respects. The service was presided over by G. Raymond Booth of the Society of Friends, Toronto. The pallbearers were Elsworth Rogers, Samuel Rogers, David Rogers, Dr. Allen Taylor, Harry Sedgewick, and Henry Parker. As dusk fell on that drizzly day, Edward S. Rogers, Sr., was laid to rest in Mount Pleasant Cemetery.

The companies paid their own special homage to their leader. Just prior to the funeral service, CFRB president Harry Sedgewick read a special tribute to Ted Rogers, which was broadcast over the station:

> Canadians may well be proud that the first all-electric radio in the world was made by Ted Rogers here in Toronto. Since that time, he made many outstanding contributions to the science of radio communication, and broadcasting as we know it today is heavily indebted to him. He guided the destinies of CFRB from the very outset, and Mr. Rogers was more than an executive head of this station. From his earliest years the miracle of wireless communication was his governing obsession. He was, however, to all, highly or low, kindly, generous and considerate.

CFRB next played Handel's poignant "Largo," then maintained radio silence as a mark of respect from 3:00 PM until 5:00 PM, the hours during which the funeral was taking place.

On May 10, Bert Trestrail, friend and business partner of Ted Rogers since 1925, wrote a two-page memorial letter for employees of the Canadian Radio Corporation. It included the following sentiments:

Just 14 years ago almost to the month he had perfected and introduced the world's first successful Batteryless Radio, which revolutionized radio reception. In a world of doubt, dire prophecies and misgivings, he formed the foundation of what eventually developed into the largest organization of its type in Canada.

His activities were many and varied. The radio factory, the tube plant and the broadcasting station will stand as monuments to his memory and tributes to his useful genius. They are accomplishments which were branded as "utterly impossible" by the outstanding engineers and laboratories at the time of their inception. "Ted" will always be remembered as a shy, modest and unassuming young genius, who, at our conventions and meetings, could barely be persuaded to rise and accept, with a bow, the tribute of his admirers.

One can well imagine the dark mood that would have hung like a storm cloud over the radio plant and the CFRB studios during the following weeks. However, his colleagues and employees knew that Ted would have wanted them to persevere and not devote much time to grief, so they quickly resumed their tasks, confident in the knowledge that they were carrying on his work.

Although his passing was sudden and completely unanticipated, Ted Rogers did have the wherewithal to provide for his beloved wife and son should such a situation occur. Although he was a hard-working businessman who spent most of his daytime hours at his office, and the majority of his free time thinking about work, he was also a proud family man who took his role as husband, father, and "provider" very seriously. The estate was settled and the will probated by the end of the month, and Velma and Ted Jr. inherited about $384,243 in property, stock holdings, funds, and assets — a remarkable figure for Depression-era Canada. However, the radio manufacturing and broadcasting assets had to be sold. Financially, they would want for nothing. Velma was able to reside comfortably in the Glen Ayr Road home for the remainder of her life. But for young Ted, the loss of his father and the sale of the business were to haunt him and motivate him throughout his life.

Edward S. "Ted" Rogers, Sr., accomplished more in his thirty-eight years than most do in a lifetime. His life was cut tragically short, leaving us to wonder what other great achievements his insightful mind and gifted hands would have given Canadians and electric communication science on a global scale. Speculation can provide almost any answer, but one fact is for certain: his illustrious track record foretold other remarkable innovations and inventions. The name "Rogers" is indelibly linked to the wireless communications industry, thanks to the abilities and drive of a young visionary possessed of many gifts who invented and improved for the benefit of everyone.

Edward Rogers, Sr., at his home, 103 Poplar Plains Road in Toronto, 1922

Chapter Seven

LEGACY

Edward S. Rogers, Sr., may have departed, but his influence remains strong. Velma Rogers kept Ted Sr.'s memory alive at 405 Glen Ayr Road by leaving his basement radio laboratory as he left it for many years afterward. She displayed many mementos of the radio company and CFRB throughout the home and instilled in Ted Jr. a great pride in his father and the achievements of his lifetime. With the newspaper clippings, photographs, and other printed material she saved over the years, she helped her son create a voluminous scrapbook, which Ted Jr. has kept to this day.

Velma married prominent Toronto lawyer John W. Graham in June 1941. The two met at a military dance when John was serving as a major in the Royal Canadian Armed Corps of the Canadian Army. During World War II, he served in Canada, England, and Northwest Europe. Previously, Major Graham had served with the Governor General's Body Guard from 1930 until 1936 and the Governor General's Horse Guards from 1936 until 1939. A sister for Ted Jr. was born in 1943, Ann Taylor Graham. Following the war, John returned to his position as general counsel for the

Imperial Life Assurance Company and set about raising his stepson and daughter.

If Marconi was the "Father of Wireless" and Fessenden the "Father of Radio Programming," then Ted Rogers, Sr., may certainly be counted as its "Boy Wonder." His work and achievements rightly permit him to assume his own place among a group of international and esteemed communication heroes. Institutions and organizations have recognized Edward S. Rogers, Sr., in many ways. Ted Rogers and Rogers Radios were profiled twice at the National Museum of Science and Technology in Ottawa. And there is a Rogers Collection at the Hammond Museum of Radio in Guelph, Ontario, where Ted is also featured with Reginald Fessenden in a special display named "Radio Days" at the Guelph Civic Museum. Ted Rogers and "The Heritage of Ted Rogers' Tube Collection" were featured in the Electronics Hall of Fame Display at the International Electronics 1969 Conference and Exposition in Toronto. The Institute of Electrical and Electronics Engineers Canada Inc. launched a special Millennium Internet site, which included a special "Achievements" section that featured the Alternating Current Tube and an accompanying essay about Ted Rogers.

Edward S. Rogers, Sr., and Velma Rogers were among the first people inducted into the Canadian Association of Broadcasters' Canadian Broadcast Hall of Fame at the association's 1982 annual convention. The honour was in recognition of their "outstanding achievements and contributions to private broadcasting and to Canada." Their names were etched into a special display at the CAB headquarters in Ottawa. When the Canadian Communications Foundation launched its Web site, Ted and Velma Rogers were recognized as "Communications Pioneers" and as such accorded special profiles that were done in conjunction with the CAB Hall of Fame.

The government and its associated bodies also recognized

Edward S. Rogers, Sr. In May 1971 he and his accomplishments were included in an exhibit titled "Famous Ontario Achievers," which was featured in the newly opened Ontario Place exhibition and amusement park on the lakeshore of Toronto. In October 1979, E. S. Rogers and Rogers Batteryless Radios were part of a special symposium titled "Canadian Inventions and Discoveries" hosted by the Ontario Science Centre. Rogers Radio Tubes were featured in a special collage poster entitled "Great Moments in Ontario: Celebrating Our Bi-Centennial." A circa 1938 Rogers Radio Tube advertisement featuring a diagram of a tube with the script "The First Successful A/C Tube" was included in the poster, produced by the office of Premier William Davis in January 1984. The Government of Ontario launched a Web site in May 1999 that included a section called "Great Moments in Ontario." Ted Rogers, Sr., and Rogers Batteryless Radios were profiled. The Toronto Historical Board erected a memorial plaque at 49 Nanton Avenue, the boyhood home of Edward S. Rogers, Sr., and Canada Post designed a special stamp honouring Edward S. Rogers, Sr., the Rogers A/C Tube, and the Rogers Batteryless Radio. These tributes by his city, his province, and his nation give due honour to Edward S. Rogers, Sr., and his inventions.

Ted Rogers was discussed in no less than fifty-one articles appearing in newspapers, magazines, and books between 1941 and 1999. He was recognized in *The Canadian Encyclopedia,* named one of "The 100 Most Important Canadians in History" in a special edition of *Maclean's* magazine, and featured in "Great Moments in Canadian Capitalism 1900 – 1999" published in *The Financial Post* magazine. When the Internet became a popular form of computer-based media, Ted Rogers could be found on eight Web sites – meaning that even in an age of microchips and satellites his contributions to communication some seventy-five years before still held enough merit to be celebrated in the modern era.

The Rogers Radio companies forged on following the loss of the man who not only brought them into existence but also inspired their greatest achievements. Shortly after Mr. Rogers' death, Bert Trestrail assumed his seat on the board of directors of Rogers Majestic/CRC. In February 1941, acting on the advice of her brother-in-law Elsworth, Velma parted with her holdings in her late husband's business enterprises. Rogers Majestic (1941) Ltd., as it was known, the Canadian Radio Corporation, and CFRB were in turn sold to British Rediffusion Inc., a communications company headquartered in London, England. W. C. Thorton Cran was appointed president of Rogers-Majestic by BRI, and Elsworth Rogers vacated the radio plant to become vice-president of CFRB. The station was separated from the radio manufacturing business at this time and managed by the newly formed Rogers Radio Broadcasting Company. Following the war, Rogers-Majestic was managed by Philips Electronics Canada, which produced radios, stereos, televisions, and appliances under that name until late 1964, when the brand was discontinued.

Ted Rogers, Jr., pursued a career in broadcasting. In 1959, while still articling with the Tory law firm, and with the encouragement and assistance of his stepfather, the twenty-six-year-old Ted partnered with Canadian media personality Joel Aldred and newspaper publisher John Bassett to create Baton-Aldred-Rogers Broadcasting. Months later, Baton applied to the federal department of communications to establish a television station in Toronto. Suitably impressed by the threesome, the government granted Baton a licence, and CFTO-TV, which stood as the first private television station in Toronto, conducted its inaugural telecast on New Year's Day 1961. The signal was broadcast from a massive 800-foot tower from studios in the small community of Agincourt, north of Toronto. It was the realization of the prediction Ted Rogers, Sr., had made in the July 1934 *Toronto Telegram* interview when he discussed the possibility of television.

In the summer of that year, Ted Jr. became aware of a radio station in Toronto that was available for purchase. He acquired CHFI-FM on November 1, 1960, for $85,000. It was the base on which all his communications assets would be built in future years. CHFI, the first FM station in Canada, began broadcasting in February 1957. At that time, FM radio was considered a novelty, and its penetration within the radio marketplace was minimal, primarily because FM receivers were large and expensive. Ted Rogers, Jr., managed CHFI even while a law student and soon contracted with Westinghouse Canada to manufacture stylish tabletop FM stereo radios based on his design. Each set was emblazoned with the CHFI-FM logo, and the phrase "98.1 – Canada's First Station for Fine Music" in the top right corner. To ensure that listeners could find CHFI easily, there was a red dot on the tuning dial to mark the exact location of the station. Each set represented a miniature billboard for CHFI. They were introduced at the 1961 CNE – the same venue used by E. S. Rogers, Sr., to launch Rogers Batteryless Radios in 1925. With these easily accessible radios and the high quality of music broadcast by the station, FM quickly gained in popularity and CHFI became a great success. The highly encouraging results prompted Ted Rogers, Jr., to establish CHFI-AM in August 1962 to further enlarge his audience. CHFI-AM carried FM quality music over the AM band to introduce people to "what they are missing" on FM. This was the first time in Canadian radio history that FM programming could be received on the AM dial. In 1990 this station became 680News and held the distinction of being the first all-news radio station in Canada.

In 1967, Ted Rogers, Jr., recognized the potential cable television held and formed Rogers Cable TV, with the slogan "Your Eye on Entertainment." This enterprise was the fourth cable firm formed in Toronto and was managed by Rogers Broadcasting, the parent company of the radio stations. In July, he acquired Bramalea Telecable Limited in Brampton, Ontario, and the 300 subscribers there were the first to be serviced by Rogers Cable. Ted Jr. was able to secure the prime locations of East York and the downtown core of Toronto for his cable operation, and in June 1968 Rogers Cable TV went on-air in the city. The company offered ten channels as well as the option of hearing music from CHFI and CKEY-AM through the cable lines. In 1971 Rogers was the first to offer cable converter boxes to the city of Toronto, and later the first to launch twenty channels. Rogers Cable TV acquired other small cable operations in outlying regions and in January 1979 scored a major advancement when it obtained majority stock in Canadian Cablesystems Limited. It was the second largest cable company in Canada with 470,000 subscribers. When combined with the subscribers already being served by Rogers Cable, the grand total came to 700,000. Seventeen months later, the company acquired Premiere Cablevision of Vancouver. It was the largest cable television operation in Canada and made Rogers Cablesystems the premier cable provider in the nation.

In 1983, Ted Rogers was a partner in a consortium whose intent was to establish a radio-telephone company in Canada. On July 1, 1985, the Cantel cellular telephone network went active. Subsequently, control was assumed by the Rogers Companies. People now had the luxury of portable personal communication and could talk while driving or walking down the street. Rogers Cantel Stores soon appeared in business centres across the nation. In 1989 the company expanded to offer Paging Services, and in 1991 began to provide high-speed data transmissions. Later, Rogers Cantel allied with American Telephone and Telegraph to form the brand Cantel-AT&T.

By 1994 Rogers Cable subscribers had access to the Internet via cable lines rather than conventional telephone lines. This allowed people to download material and obtain information much faster than before. Originally named Cable-Link, this division was renamed Rogers Wave and then Rogers@Home. That same year Ted Rogers acquired Maclean Hunter Limited and added magazine and newspaper publishing to his telecommunications empire while at the same time increasing his cable television and paging subscriber base. As the 1990s came to a close, British Telecom and AT&T made a joint investment in Rogers Cantel, and Microsoft made an investment in Rogers Communications and struck a partnership with Rogers Cable to bring interactive television to Canada.

Beginning with a small radio station with limited revenue and an even smaller audience, Ted Rogers, Jr., built a national telecommunications company that is renowned the world over for its technological advances and innovations. The parent firm, which directs three operating companies managing media and Internet interests, cable systems, and wireless communication, is, fittingly, incorporated under the name Rogers Communications.

Ted Rogers appreciates that he owes much of his success to his father and pays tribute to him in many ways. A four-foot oil portrait of Edward S. Rogers, Sr., was commissioned in 1957 and has always held a place of honour in Ted Rogers' residence, either above the mantel in the dining room, or in the library. During the late 1960s, Ted began assembling a collection of Rogers Batteryless and Rogers-Majestic radios. They provide a link to his father and are displayed both at his home and in the lobbies of various Rogers business offices.

In May 1975, Ted Rogers presented the first Ted Rogers, Sr./Velma Rogers Graham Award at the annual convention of the Canadian Association of Broadcasters. This award was designed to recognize the person making the most significant contribution in a single continuing fashion to the Canadian broadcasting system and for exceptional community service in the role of a broadcaster. The award rotates annually between the Canadian Association of Broadcasters and the Canadian Cable Television Association.

Thirteen months after this award made its debut, The Edward S. "Ted" Rogers, Sr., Fellowship in the Faculty of Applied Science and Engineering was established by Ted Rogers, Jr., at the University of Toronto. This fund provides donations to graduate students for research and study in the field of telecommunications. The fellowship was first awarded in the fall of 1988, and on the tenth anniversary of its presentation, a certificate was created to accompany the cheques given to the three winning scholars.

Ted Rogers, Jr., established another connection between education and his father's name when in January 1989 he made a substantial donation to the Ryerson Polytechnic Institute in Toronto for faculty improvements as part of their Pride and Purpose campaign. Two years later, the Rogers Communications Centre opened its doors at a gala Celebration of Progress event. This twenty-five million dollar facility was dedicated to the memory of Edward S. Rogers, Sr. It stands as a 113,000-square-foot three-storey facility at 80 Gould Street and houses the schools of Radio and Television Arts, Image Arts, Computer Science, and Journalism, ready to serve 1,500 students. It is also home to the Ontario Press Council, the studios of the student-operated radio station, CJRT, and forty radio and television production studios.

Faculties and facilities moved into the new and architecturally impressive building over the spring and summer, and The Rogers Communications Centre accepted its first students in September 1992. The RCC has gone on to become the premier facility in Canada for degrees, research, and professional development in the creation of electronic media and digital communications.

In January 1997, the Rogers Centre launched a new endeavour of which its namesake would be proud. One blustery winter's day,

SPIRIT went on the air. The name is an acronym for "Student Produced Internet Radio and Interactive Technology." The station broadcasts over the Internet twenty-four hours a day with eight hours of content in a continual loop. SPIRIT offers the most extensive programming of any Internet station within a Canadian university. Internet radio was a relatively new phenomenon at the station's inception, much like telegraphy was some eighty years earlier. 3BP and SPIRIT thus share more than one common link.

Whenever Ted Rogers, Jr., has the opportunity, he will speak about his father with fond admiration. "He invented the first ever all-electric 'batteryless' radio in the world!" Ted Jr. comments with the enthusiasm that only a son can have for his father. "He worked hard and was able to bring people together who had good ideas, then motivate them. And he was patriotic. He had the chance to move to the United States with his invention, where he could have made more money, but he chose to stay in Canada and make opportunities here."

At a gala celebration on June 21, 1971 – the seventy-first anniversary of the birthday of Edward S. Rogers, Sr. – CHFI-AM was renamed CFTR to represent Canada's First Ted Rogers. When CFTR released a record album some months later, the jacket stated:

> Every time we plug our radios in to our wall socket and with the flick of a dial enjoy today's popular music, news and sports programmes, we have reason to be grateful to the late Ted Rogers. He not only initiated this kind of programming in Canada, but equally as important, he made it possible for everyone to have easy access to radio receivers, by inventing the world's first A/C vacuum tube. With this new invention, out went the big, bulky batteries that had previously powered radios, and in came the World's first "batteryless" station right here in Toronto. So you can see there was no better day of the

year than June 21 for CFTR's Ted Rogers to honour his illustrious father, and pledge to you, the listener, that the same pioneering spirit that started back in the '20s will continue in the '70s at the new CFTR.

In December 1998, it was discovered that 545 Lakeshore Boulevard West, the current home of the offices and studios of Rogers Broadcasting television station CFMT, was known as Rogers Radio Plant #2 from 1938 until 1946. This same building served both father and son in their business pursuits. It is the last remaining structure that produced Rogers Radios because the plants at 90 Chestnut Street and 622 Fleet Street were torn down to make way for new buildings.

The legacy of Edward Samuel Rogers, Sr., takes on many forms and can be found in a variety of different sources. Any time anyone turns on a radio that is plugged into a wall they are in effect paying homage to Rogers and his invention. The family and business heritage that has been recognized by government at all levels and institutions of several types owes its collective gratitude to a tousle-haired youngster from a good family. Ted Rogers, Sr., followed his imagination and dreamed. He developed his skills with steadfast determination and matured into a tremendously successful entrepreneur of national calibre. While doing all this, he revolutionized home entertainment for the benefit of everyone along the way. The radio wizard who is Edward S. Rogers, Sr., stands as an inspiration to anyone with a dream who possesses the ability to act on ideas and can aspire to success.

NEW WAY

OLD WAY

The "spray-shield" tube shown at right above, is the latest great radio development. A metal film is blasted right into the glass surface and over the base thus providing the ONLY perfect shield and making it possible to discard the old-type shielding can (shown at left) which permitted of vibration, distortion and over heating. Spray-Shield Tubes afford greatly improved reception, longer life of tubes at no extra cost.

Look at the TUBES in a radio
Insist on "SPRAY-SHIELD" TUBES
found only in
Rogers - Majestic - De Forest Crosley

Sources

July 1913

Toronto Telegram, "Toronto Boys' Wireless Caught Story of Wreck in Ireland"

December 1921

The Toronto Star, "Newmarket Wireless 'Talks' to Scotland"

The Toronto Star Weekly, "Wireless Wizard Has Performed Big Feat"

The Newmarket Era, "Wireless Wizard Telegraphs from Newmarket"

January, February 1922

QST, Connecticut "Transatlantic Tests Succeed!"

September 1922

The Toronto Star, "Newmarket Station Heard in Scotland: Feat of Edward Rogers Has Never Been Duplicated"

December 1923

The Toronto Star, "Local Radio Fan Relays Message to MacMillan's Ship in the Arctic"

The Globe, "Amateur Establishes New Radio Record: Successful in Holding Conversation with England"

November 1925

The Globe, "Develops New Type of Radio Receiver"

December 1925

Radio, "A Romance in Radio: Rogers Batteryless Sets Creates New Standard in Radio Principles and Reception"

November 1926

Radio News of Canada, "The History and Development of Rogers Batteryless Receiving Sets"

February 1927
   The Globe, "Has Directed Building of Batteryless Station"
March 1927
   The New York Times, "Station CFRB and E.S. Rogers"
   Radio Trade Builder, "Radio Trade Notes – E.S. Rogers"
January 1928
   The Globe, "To Listen at Sea"
   The Toronto Telegram, "CFRB to Broadcast Midnight Program Sunday for
   Ted Rogers on Aquitania"
1928
   Who's Who in Canada 1928–29
October 1928
   Radio Trade Builder, "Rogers Batteryless and Majestic Amalgamate for Canada –
   Rogers, The Inventor"
August 1928
   The Globe, "Batteryless Set Credit Is Given Young Canadian"
September 1928
   The Globe, "Rogers Is Hailed as Pioneer Inventor of Batteryless Set"
March 1929
   Radio Trade Builder, "Standard Radio Corporation Erecting Large Factory"
   The Globe, "Completes Big Deal – E.S. Rogers links CFRB to CBS"
April 1929
   "CFRB Toronto, Station and Artists" booklet by CFRB
   The Globe, "New Radio Factory Going Up on Fleet Street"
June 1929
   The Globe, "Canada's Most Modern Radio Factory Soon to Start
   Production"
   The Globe, "Rogers' New Radio Plant Is Impressive Gesture of Canadian
   Enterprise"
March 1930
   The Globe, "A Romance of Radioland: E. S. Rogers and His Bride"
April 1930
   The Toronto Telegram, "Recently Married: Mr. and Mrs. E. S. Rogers"
July 1930
   The Globe, "The Man Whose Genius Created Batteryless Radio"
   The Globe, "Better and Better Broadcasting Assures Radio of Greater Future
   While New Receivers Keep Pace"
November 1930
   The Globe, "Batteryless Set Given World by Young Canadian"
   The Globe, "CFRB New Studios Opened in Grand Display"
July 1932
   Radio and Electrical Home Equipment, "E. S. Rogers Elected President of
   Rogers-Majestic"

September 1932
  The Mail and Empire, "Radio Talks"
April 1933
  The Globe, "The Giant Voice of the Dominion – New Towers Over Which
  CFRB's 10,000 Watt Signal Goes Out"
  The Toronto Telegram, "New CFRB Masts"
  The Toronto Star Weekly, "From a Hobby to a Big Business"
May 1933
  The Toronto Telegram, "Character from Handwriting – E.S. Rogers"
November 1933
  The Globe, "Early Prediction Made by Inventor Finally Realized"
February 1934
  The Globe, "Builders of Greater Toronto"
June 1934
  The Toronto Telegram, "News! Hot from the Spot: A Dip into the Future with
  the Youthful Radio Wizard Whose Early Housetop Aerial Was the
  Forerunner of a Great House of Wonder"
September 1934
  Torontonian Society Blue Book
February 1934
  The Globe, "Pioneer of A-C Set"
December 1935
  The Globe, "E. S. Rogers and Rogers Metal Spray Tubes"
February 1937
  CFRB 10th Anniversary Yearbook
May 1939
  Obituaries in every Toronto newspaper, and *Variety* magazine
October 1941
  Canadian Radio Data Book, "Rungs in the Ladder of Radio History"
September 1944
  Rogers Ultron Tubes Data Book, "The History of Rogers Electronic Tubes is a
  Record of Achievement"
August 1948
  Canadian Broadcaster, "9RB Calling"
February 1952
  CFRB 25th Anniversary Book
February 1957
  Monumentous Years: The Story of CFRB 1927–1957 (record album by CFRB)
  The Toronto Telegram, "The Canadian Who Led the World... CFRB Result of
  Toronto Man's Genius"
October 1959
  Rogers–Majestic advertisement, "It All Started When Ted Rogers Made
  Batteries Old Fashioned"

September 1960
Canadian Electronics Workshop, "CFRB: Spanning 33 Years of Canadian Broadcasting"

June 1965
The Toronto Telegram, "In Blackburn's View: Ted Rogers, Sr. and CFRB"

September 1966
"Edward Samuel Rogers' Collection – A Canadian Heritage: The Distinguished Edward Samuel Rogers' Collection of Electronic Tubes" (booklet by CHFI-FM)

August 1967
Toronto

November 1967
Ideas in Exile: A History of Canadian Invention

May 1968
Inventors: Great Ideas in Canadian Enterprise"
From Spark to Space: The Story of Amateur Radio in Canada

July 1969
Electron, "The Canadian Radio Pioneer: Ted Rogers and the Batteryless Radio"

October 1969
International Electronics Conference and Exposition, Toronto: Electronics Hall of Fame display (The Heritage of Ted Rogers' Tube Collection)

May 1970
Electron, "More on the Rogers Story"

May 1971
Ontario Place, "Famous Ontario Achievers"

August 1971
CFTR: Sounds Familiar (record album)

January 1972
St. James, "Ted Rogers and the Batteryless Radio"

February 1972
CHFI 15th Anniversary Event, "The Rogers Legacy: It Can Be Done"
CHFI print advertisement, "It Can Be Done: E. S. Ted Rogers 1925, E.S. Ted Rogers, Jr. 1972"

February 1974
Simpson's Department Store advertisement, "Ted Rogers' Invention"

May 1975
Ted Rogers, Sr./Velma Rogers Graham Award established at CAB

January 1976
The CAB Story 1926 – 1976, Private Broadcasting in Canada

April 1976
"Edward S. 'Ted' Rogers, Sr. Fellowship in the Faculty of Applied Science and Engineering" established at the University of Toronto

July 1976

  Colombo, John Robert, *Colombo's Canadian References*

February 1977

  Rogers. Radio's Pioneering Family (plaque by CHFI-FM)

July 1977

  The Story of CFRB: Sinc, Betty and the Morning Man

September 1977

  The Saga of The Vacuum Tube

September 1979

  Straight Up: Private Broadcasting in Canada 1918–1958

October 1979

  Ontario Science Centre, "Canadian Inventions and Discoveries"

June 1982

  70 Years of Radio Tubes and Valves,

  Signing On: The Birth of Radio in Canada

September 1983

  Debrett's Illustrated Guide to the Canadian Establishment

January 1984

  A Toronto Almanac: In Celebration of Toronto's 150th Anniversary

  "Great Moments in Ontario: Celebrating Our Bi-Centennial" (poster)

April 1984

  Rogers Annual Report, 1983, "Building a Home Entertainment Industry

January 1985

  From Coast to Coast: A Personal History of Radio

July 1985

  Report on Business, "The High-Wire Act of Ted Rogers"

January 1986

  Horizons Canada, "Discoveries and Inventions"

May 1987

  Connections, "Broadcasting Miracle"

September 1987

  Memorial Plaque by Toronto Historical Board at 49 Nanton Avenue,
  boyhood home of Edward S. Rogers, Sr.

May 1988

  The Canadian Encyclopedia.

September 1988

  The Collins Dictionary of Canadian History: 1867–Present

November 1988

  Canada: From Sea to Sea

May 1990

  Junior Encyclopedia of Canada

September 1990

  The Toronto Story

Spring 1992
  Rapport
April 1992
  National Museum of Science and Technology, Ottawa, *Radio Communication in Canada: A Historical and Technological Survey*
September 1992
  Canada Firsts: A Salute to Canada and Canadian Achievements
May 1993
  CFRB program, "Ted Rogers' Radio History"
October 1993
  Too Good to Be True: Toronto in the 1920's
March 1994
  Maclean's, "King of the Road"
October 1994
  Pathfinders: Canadian Tributes, "Edward Samuel Rogers: Plugging in the World"
November 1994
  Toronto Sketches 3: The Way We Were
March 1995
  "Connexions" exhibit in National Museum of Science and Technology, Ottawa (features 1925 Rogers Batteryless Radio model 100/ text card on ESR Sr.)
September 1995
  Ted Rogers,
December 1995
  "Canadian Communications Foundation – CAB Hall of Fame" Web site: rcc.ryerson.ca/schools/rta/ccf
February 1997
  CFRB "The Ted Woloshyn Show"
March 1997
  "E. S. Rogers: The Man" and "E. S. Rogers: The Companies" articles in 'The Loudspeaker' newsletter published by the Ottawa Vintage Radio Club 'E. S. Rogers' CFRB Web site: cfrb.istar.ca/profiles/pro_esrogers. html
July 1998
  Maclean's, "The 100 Most Important Canadians in History"
August 1998
  CKCO-TV, "This Day In History"
December 1998
  "Radio Days Gone By: An Exhibit about Early Radio and E. S. Rogers, Sr., the Inventor of the Batteryless Radio" (museum exhibit, Elman W. Campbell Museum, Newmarket)
February 1999
  "The Rogers Collection" Hammond Museum of Radio, Guelph Web site: kwarc.org/hammond/rogers.html

March 1999

    CFMT Television Interstitial "Rogers Radio Invention"

April 1999

    Visual Convergence, "The Canadian Contributions to Communications"

May 1999

    "Radio Days" exhibit at Guelph Civic Museum, Guelph

    "Great Moments in Ontario – Ontario 2000," Government of Ontario Web site: ontario.2000.on.ca./english/greatmoments/scitech/radio

    Free-for-All: The Struggle for Dominance on the Digital Frontier

June 1999

    The Financial Post, "Great Moments in Canadian Capitalism 1900–1999"

    The Canadian Establishment: Volume 3: The Titans

August 1999

    "The Rhythm of History: Musical Memories of the CNE" exhibit, Canadian National Exhibition

    Toronto Life, "Urban Decoder"

    Mount Pleasant Cemetery: An Illustrated Guide

September 1999

    "The Rogers Collection" exhibit of Rogers Batteryless Radios within the Hammond Museum of Radio, Guelph

October 1999

    Forum, Ryerson Polytechnic University newspaper, "New Stamp to Honour Rogers Centre Namesake"

    Newmarket Era-Banner, "Celebrate 2000: A Look at the Community's Past, Present and Future"

    CBC Television, "Life and Times" – "Ambition: The Life and Times of Ted Rogers"

    Broadcast Dialogue, "Interactive TV Means the Best Is Yet to Come!" by Ted Rogers, Jr

December 1999

    "Achievements – Alternating Current Tube," Institute of Electronics and Electronics Engineers, Web site: ieee.ca/millennium

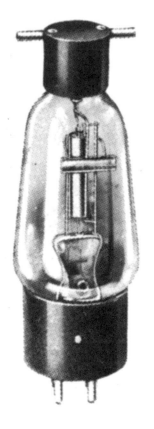

Rogers A / C Tube Type 32

Index

250
MA

RFC

RF